Midwife Crisis

The calamities of a trainee midwife

Hilary Cotterill

MONARCH
BOOKS

Oxford, UK and Grand Rapids, Michigan, USA

Copyright © Hilary Cotterill 2005.
The right of Hilary Cotterill to be identified
as author of this work has been asserted by her in
accordance with the Copyright, Designs
and Patents Act 1988.

First published in the UK in 2005 by Monarch Books
(a publishing imprint of Lion Hudson plc),
Mayfield House, 256 Banbury Road, Oxford OX2 7DH
Tel: +44 (0) 1865 302750   Fax: +44 (0) 1865 302757
Email: monarch@lionhudson.com
www.lionhudson.com

Distributed by:
UK: Marston Book Services Ltd, PO Box 269,
Abingdon, Oxon OX14 4YN
USA: Kregel Publications, PO Box 2607,
Grand Rapids, Michigan 49501

ISBN-13: 978 1 85424 729 2 (UK)
ISBN-10: 1 85424 729 8 (UK)
ISBN-13: 978 0 8254 6097 5 (USA)
ISBN-10: 0 8254 6097 2 (USA)

Unless otherwise stated, Scripture quotations are
taken from the Holy Bible, New International Version,
copyright © 1973, 1978, 1984 by the International Bible Society.
Used by permission of Hodder and Stoughton Ltd.
All rights reserved.

British Library Cataloguing Data
A catalogue record for this book is available
from the British Library.

Cover illustrations by David Mostyn

Printed and bound in Great Britain by
Cox & Wyman Ltd, Reading, Berkshire

Dedication

Dedicated to the loves of my life, Adrian, Peter, David and Jonathan, and my father Donald John.

Acknowledgments

I would like to thank all those friends and family, whose love, care and prayerful support helped us through the darkest times, especially Adrian's parents, Bill and Dorothy. My thanks also to Tony Collins and all at Monarch for their dedication, professionalism and encouragement.

Disclaimer: All patient and staff names are fictional, having been changed to protect the identities of the individuals concerned.

Chapter One

The bus driver's eyes bulged and his knees buckled as he attempted to lift the metal trunk up the steps.

"What on earth 'ave you got in 'ere?"

I pushed the trunk for all I was worth and we somehow managed to wrestle the unwilling object into submission amongst the other passengers' shopping and folding pushchairs. He stood upright and pointedly rubbed his lower back for a few seconds. I smiled sweetly.

"Thank you so much for your help. I couldn't have done this without you."

He sighed the deep sigh of the man who regrets offering help, swung himself into his seat, and shut the doors. I found a seat where I could keep a good eye on the trunk, but could still feel the probing eyes of the other passengers as they considered whether any of their belongings were in mortal danger from this over-sized piece of luggage.

The bus pulled out of Watford Bus Station, and we slowly swung our way towards Welwyn Garden City, some 17 miles away. This was it, the beginning of the next phase of my nursing career, and I felt a mixture of excitement and trepidation.

I was going to begin my midwifery training after four demanding years in Edinburgh where I had trained and worked for a year as a staff nurse. I was filled with a mixture of nervousness and confidence. The former because this was all so new – a new job, a new hospital, even a new country – and the latter because I was bringing with me experiences of immensely difficult and demanding times, and yet, by the Grace of God, I had survived.

The bus pulled into its stop, and the driver stared stoically ahead as I manhandled the trunk and my suitcase rather clumsily down the steps. The doors closed and the bus pulled away, and I was left staring at the hospital which loomed in front of me.

Unlike the Royal Infirmary of Edinburgh, which is steeped in centuries of tradition, this hospital, the Queen Elizabeth II, was modern and multi-storey. There was a large car park which I crossed, pulling the trunk on its tiny wheels. I eventually arrived at the reception desk and waited to be acknowledged by a young blonde woman who was reading a magazine.

"Good afternoon. I'm one of the new student midwives, and I've been told to report here to find where my room is in the Nurses' Home."

Blondie yawned and reluctantly lifted herself out of her black plastic chair. "Follow me." We trundled out of the double doors and back across the car park. "Go up there. That's where you'll find your room."

I followed her pointing finger and tried not to grimace as a very large flight of stairs came into view. Unsure as to whether it was safe to leave the trunk unattended, I heaved it up to the first floor and wandered along the corridor in search of an office.

"You're in the wrong building. It's that one over on the other side of the car park – Harmer House. You're in Room 17, on the first floor."

I smiled my thanks and then proceeded to drag the luggage all the way back down the stairs. I wondered why it was called Harmer House – it seemed a very inappropriate name for nurses and midwives. Back across the car park I went, and then up another two flights of stairs. I followed the uncarpeted corridor along to the end, and found Room 17 on the right-hand side. By the time I reached my destination my arms felt as though they were parting company with the rest of me, and my hands were trembling as I tried to put the key in the lock.

It's always an exciting moment when you enter a new home, and I was excited and hopeful as the door opened. Inside, there was a bed in one corner and a desk under the window. At the other end was a wardrobe and washbasin. But it was the colour and odour which struck me more than anything. The walls and ceiling were the colour of old tobacco, and the curtains were pungent with the smell of stale cigarettes.

I opened the window and let the outside air flow into the musty room. Sitting on the bed, I drew up a plan of action; after a couple of minutes, I emptied all my belongings into the cupboards and drawers, then set to with a basin full of water and detergent and washed all the ceiling and the walls. I fell into bed exhausted, but full of anticipation.

The night which followed was spent wriggling and jumping at every unfamiliar sound. But when the morning came, I was up bright and early and ready to begin the new course. The midwifery school was situated on the sixth floor of the hospital, and I made my way there in good time for the nine o'clock start.

When I arrived, there was already one other student sitting in the classroom. "Is this the midwifery classroom?" I asked, more to initiate a conversation than anything else.

The young woman turned around in her seat. "If it isn't, then I'm in the wrong place." She smiled and held out her hand. "Hi, I'm Jennifer." We shook hands, and I sat down next to her.

"Have you had far to travel?" I asked.

"No, I live in Harpenden, so it's only about 20 minutes in the car."

"I'm in the Nurses' Home, so it's even less for me."

"How is it there?"

"Well, you know what Nurses' Homes are like."

Jennifer grimaced, "Indeed I do, you poor thing!"

Just then, a couple more students entered the room. "Is this the right place for the midwifery training?" they asked. I was struck by their soft Irish accents. Jennifer and I reassured them that this was the place, and they sat down behind us.

Sinead and Moira were just making themselves comfortable when Abigail arrived. She walked in with her arms full of folders, pencil case and a huge wad of lined paper. As she was passing the back row of desks, she caught her heel on one of the chair legs and, losing her balance, sent the folders, pencil case and paper in a myriad of directions which would have been the envy of any aerobatic display team.

"Oh dear!" she said. "I knew I should have worn flat shoes today." Jennifer, Sinead, Moira and I all scrambled around on the floor collecting the far-flung items. At this precise moment, our tutor, Miss Harrier, arrived.

"Good morning, ladies. I must say that I didn't expect to find you all on your knees so early in the day!"

We clambered back to our desks in unison, and tried to establish some degree of decorum. Abigail sat at the front with Jennifer and myself. Miss Harrier looked at her watch. It was two minutes to nine. As we sat in dutiful silence my attention wandered to a diagram of the female reproductive system, and then to a rather odd-looking model of a pelvis with what looked like a knitted sock dangling from it. I'd never seen anything quite like that in real life, and it had me quite perplexed.

A moment later, three other students arrived. "Sorry we're late. We couldn't find anywhere to park. It's murder at this time of day."

"Very well. It's Helen, Zoe and Denise, isn't it?"

"Yes, Miss Harrier."

"That's fine. Just sit anywhere. When you are settled, we will begin with the introductions."

The moment took me back four years to when I had sat in that classroom in Edinburgh, staring out of the window at the endless snow, and wondering what lay ahead. Now, in contrast, the sun was shining, and instead of being in a huge room with 30 other students, there were only eight of us here, and the atmosphere was altogether less formal.

I was disturbed from my daydream by Miss Harrier's voice. "Hilary, will you please stand up and introduce yourself to the group? Just say a little about where you completed your nursing training, and any post-registration experience you have had."

"Oh dear," I said. "Um, well, I trained at the Royal Infirmary of Edinburgh, and worked as a staff nurse in Oral Surgery and Coronary Care for a year after qualifying." I sat down again hastily in case anyone should ask any questions. Public speaking was really not my thing. We went round the group and I discovered that several of the girls had come from large teaching hospitals in London, and that Sinead and Moira had come all the way from Dublin.

With the introductions complete, Miss Harrier proceeded to embark upon various legal issues associated with midwifery, and a brief guide to the history of the profession. By coffee time my left hand was complaining of writer's cramp. I hadn't taken notes like this for over a year, and wished that I had persevered with learning shorthand.

The shot of caffeine revived us all. We had been used to working in busy and demanding areas of nursing, and it was difficult to get used to sitting still for such long periods of time. We took a walk downstairs to the department which distributed uniforms, and we admired one another in the blue-and-white check dresses which would depict the humble nature of our new role. I think that we all shuddered inwardly as we realised that we were returning to the bottom of the pile once again, at least until the next intake of student midwives arrived in another six months' time.

Returning to the classroom once again, we were introduced formally to the female pelvis which had been sitting coyly on Miss Harrier's desk. "You may have been wondering what this woollen appendage is?"

We nodded dumbly, not wishing to look too stupid, at least not on our first day.

"Well, it's supposed to represent the muscles surrounding the pelvic outlet, through which a baby passes when it is being born during a normal delivery." Ah, so that's what it was. Not a new line in thermals, after all.

Miss Harrier then talked a little about the three stages of labour, and in the afternoon, we learned more about hormones. By the end of the day, the "Danger, your brain has now reached overload" light was flash-

ing on my mental stressometer, and it was a considerable relief to leave the classroom at half past four.
Walking out into the spring sunshine, I crossed the car
park and returned to my room. I dropped the day's
notes onto the bed, grabbed my handbag and a shopping bag, and headed for the town.

It was a novelty to find everywhere so flat after
Edinburgh's steep and imposing hills. All the buildings
were comparatively modern, and this also was in stark
contrast to the centuries of history embodied in the
stone buildings of the Scottish capital. The roads in
Welwyn were pleasant and lined with trees, and the trees
themselves were budding with the greenness that holds
so much promise – the hope of springtime. Edinburgh's
windswept cobbles seemed a million miles away.

As I walked along, I kept an eye open for a suitable
church. I knew how much I had relied upon the support
and friendship of other Christians in Edinburgh, and
was very aware of the fact that I couldn't face all the
challenges which lay ahead on my own.

Returning to the Nurses' Home, I went to check
out the notice boards to see if there was any information about a Hospital Christian Fellowship, or if any
churches were advertised there. In fact, I found both.
The Hospital Christian Fellowship met once a week on
a Wednesday afternoon, in one of the lounges in the
main Home, and the local Baptist church was located
about half a mile from the hospital.

Life seemed to be getting sorted out, and all that I
needed to do now was find a laundry room, and then
try to find out whether it was safe to leave anything in
the communal fridge. I eventually found the former in
the basement, and decided that I would have to take a
chance on the latter.

In spite of the novelty of my situation, and the many positive comparisons with the life I had just left in Edinburgh, I still felt lonely. All the people I loved and cared for were many miles away. I went to bed with a combination of a heavy heart and the hope that tomorrow might just be better than today.

The following morning we were all back in the classroom once again, learning about the intricacies of the hormonal control which takes place during pregnancy. It was mind-blowing stuff, and it made me think of Psalm 139 which states, "I praise you because I am fearfully and wonderfully made." It was true – such intricacy had to be the creation of a wonderful Being. For so many systems to knit together in a place in which new life can be created and nurtured – this had to be the result of more than sheer luck or chance.

In the afternoon, the theme continued as we learned about the developing embryo. As the fertilised ovum divides and divides again, so cells become differentiated to form all of the organs of the human body. How the cells should "know" what they should become seemed incredible to me, and yet they do, and the creation of each person is a miraculous thing. I found myself in awe of a God who allows people to share in the wonder of His creation in this way.

Wednesday came around and, following another fascinating day studying, I found the lounge in which the Hospital Christian Fellowship was meeting. It was a small group of five nurses and student midwives, and I felt rather conspicuous as the group's newest member. Its leader was Alicia, a student midwife in the last few months of her training. She had short, blonde hair, and her face held an expression of serenity which never seemed to change, irrespective of her situation.

"Do come in and sit down," she said, as I put my head around the door. "Have you just started here?"

"Yes, I have."

"Well, this is Debbie, Sandra, Lorna and Tess." I nodded and smiled at each girl. "Do tell us a bit about yourself."

I gave them a brief history, explaining how I had moved down from Edinburgh following four years there, and how meeting with Jesus whilst there had completely changed my life. I explained that prior to Edinburgh I had been educated in Hong Kong, and how my life had changed so dramatically from one of great material wealth to one of spiritual wealth, with rather less on the material side. They listened politely, and then Alicia went on to lead a Bible study from John's Gospel, concerning Jesus washing the disciples' feet.

That story had always spoken volumes to me. I think it's because I had come across so many feet in the previous four years. Some of them had been pleasant enough – with clean, short toenails, and nice, clean soles. But others had had nails which were overgrown from months of neglect, and nasty, smelly, ingrained dirt which seemed to remain stubbornly in place, despite water, flannel and a large bar of soap.

That Jesus should wash the feet of His disciples was such a picture of His humility. Here was the Creator of the universe, on His knees, and gently cleansing the feet of His followers who, by all accounts, were a pretty motley crew. Such love and intimacy blew my mind.

Following the study, Alicia asked me if I had found a church yet, and I explained that I had located the local Baptist church. She said that this was where she worshipped, and asked if I would like to go along with her on the following Sunday. I gratefully agreed.

Thursday and Friday involved more studying of the female reproductive organs, and included a test at the end of the week. By the end of it all, I was completely exhausted, and wondered if I would ever get to grips with all the different hormones and their effects on the body.

Saturday was spent having a lie-in, and listening to the sound of the radios of the other occupants of the Nurses' Home. The floors here were not carpeted, so every sound seemed to be amplified along the corridors. Most of the girls seemed to get along well, and I was pleased to find that Abigail had moved into a room just a couple of doors along from mine.

In keeping with everything else about her, Abigail's taste in music was exuberant and abundant. She loved brightly coloured clothes, and drove a brand new Capri which her father had purchased as a present at the beginning of her midwifery training. She loved to sing along to her music at the top of her voice, and could often be heard serenading the world at full volume from the comfort of a deep bubble bath. There were occasional mutterings by the other girls on the landing, but most people found that they couldn't help liking Abi – she was so full of warmth and good humour, that you could not remain irritated by her for very long.

Sunday came around, and I met with Alicia at the doors of the main Home. We walked to church together, and we talked about our respective weeks. Alicia told me that she was hoping to work in India as a missionary following her training, and she was in the process of sorting out visas and finding out about the necessary vaccinations she would need in preparation for her work there.

We arrived at the church, and the service was great.

14

People were very kind and welcoming, but in my heart I kept thinking back to the week I had spent at a prayer conference in Suffolk just a few months previously, when my eyes had been opened to the work and ministry of the Holy Spirit. I wondered if the Lord was leading me on to something new and different. I really didn't want to lose all that I had learned there, and I left the church wondering if I would ever be allowed again to share in the freedom of worship which had been so wonderful during that special week, which now seemed so long ago.

Chapter Two

The days of study rolled into weeks, and before long, we were allocated to our first wards. Abi and I were allocated to the antenatal ward, where we would begin to learn how to examine pregnant women at various stages of pregnancy, get to grips with fetal monitoring, and care for women who were admitted to stabilise conditions of pregnancy such as pre-eclampsia.

Abi and I were due to begin work on a late shift on the Monday afternoon. We walked onto the ward and introduced ourselves to the sister in charge. We were shown the office and proceeded to listen to the Report from the morning staff. Abi and I glanced anxiously at one another. The Report seemed to be given in another language, and we were having some difficulty deciphering all that was said. Between the "para" this and "multip" that, "primip" and "P.E.T."'s, we were rather bemused, but we kept smiling and writing it all down in our notebooks in the hope that one day it would all make perfect sense.

Sister Beaumont had noticed our grimaces, however, and she stopped in mid-flow as she mentioned the word "primip" for the fifth time.

"I know it sounds like a form of chimpanzee, but really it's not. The word refers to a woman who is pregnant for the first time."

We smiled in response, and tried to look as though we'd understood all along, but secretly we were glad of Sister's understanding.

At the end of Report, it became apparent that the postnatal ward was exceptionally busy, and as a result, several of the delivered women were occupying one of the bays in the antenatal ward. It seemed that Abi and I were about to have some postnatal experience thrown in for good measure.

Abi and I were each allocated a bay of women to look after under the careful supervision of two qualified midwives, Clarissa and Steph, who would manage the ward for the evening. We were just walking out of the office when a woman came running out of the postnatal bay, looking very anxious. "Help! Please help!" she said. "My baby has gone blue! He's stopped breathing!"

I momentarily froze. Had we covered this yet in the classroom? Nope. What was I supposed to do with a baby who was suffering a respiratory arrest? If it had happened to an adult, I would have known exactly what to do, but this was totally different. The expression on the mother's face jolted me out of this brief internal discussion. I knew I had to do something, and I followed her quickly to the cot where her motionless baby lay.

"Do something! Please do something!" Her voice was rising with her fear and panic.

"It's alright," I said, using the phrase which had been used so often in Coronary Care. "I'll just take him through to one of the midwives." Before the mother could say another word, I scooped her little son into my arms and rushed out of the bay in search of someone who would know what to do.

Miraculously, at that very moment the senior

house officer walked onto the ward. "What's the matter with that baby?" she asked.

"He's stopped breathing. Please, can you help me?"

"Take him into the treatment room; there's a resuscitation trolley set up in there."

I followed her pointing finger, and carried the little baby into the room and bundled him onto the trolley. The action of putting him down seemed to stimulate him, and I stood watching in disbelief as he began to squirm, and his colour changed from a dusky purple to a healthy pink once again. A moment later he began to snuffle and then, to my great relief, began to cry. "Oh, thank God," I muttered. "He gave me an awful fright."

"I can see that," said the doctor, who was standing behind me. She undressed the baby and listened to his heart and lungs with her stethoscope. "He seems alright now. It must just have been one of those things. Some babies do this, you know. It was good that his mother noticed. Tell her we'll take him up to Special Care, just to observe him closely for a couple of days, but hopefully, he should be fine."

I could have hugged her. "Thank you so much," I said. In spite of my relief, I hated the feeling of inadequacy, and had to keep telling myself that one day, hopefully, I might just know how to handle all these eventualities without feeling so stupid.

I returned the little boy to his mother, who was understandably very tearful. A few minutes later, she was taking her little son upstairs to the Special Care Baby Unit, reassured in the knowledge that he would have round-the-clock observation there, should anything similar happen again.

As they disappeared from the ward, Abi sauntered out of her bay. "Alright, Hil?" she asked casually, totally unaware of my hair-raising introduction to midwifery. "It's nice here, isn't it? No dramas, just talking to a load of women who are anticipating the happiest days of their lives." She sighed contentedly. "Yep, I think I'm going to love it here."

I smiled to myself, and thought that I might just love it here too, as long as my patients had the decency to keep breathing. I spent the remainder of my shift keeping an extra-vigilant eye on the babies in the cots by the side of their mothers' beds. Just in case.

By the end of the first week, Abi and I were invited to attend the weekly ward round with the most senior consultant obstetrician, Mr Woodehouse. We were both oblivious to the fact that one of his pet hobbies was putting student midwives on the spot. Consequently, Abi and I stood happily behind all the registrars, senior house officers and medical students, lulled into a false sense of security that we would be here to watch and learn from the great man himself.

Miss Harrier, and our clinical tutor, Mrs Dickinson, had also brought the other six girls from our course along for good measure. It came as a terrifying shock, therefore, when Mr Woodehouse turned directly to me and said, "You there. Come and palpate this woman's abdomen for me and tell me what you find."

I saw everyone's eyes turn in my direction. He couldn't mean me. I'd only just started. I looked pleadingly across to Miss Harrier, hoping that she would speak up on my behalf. Instead, she just smiled reassuringly and nodded her head in the direction of the unfortunate patient who sat waiting expectantly in her bed. She was a new admission, and I hadn't had the opportunity to examine her previously.

I could feel the blush of embarrassment gathering

momentum with each second that passed. I looked at Abi, and she just smiled in return. There was nothing for it; I was going to have to do this, in front of all these people. I moved slowly towards the bed.

What did I need to do first? Oh yes, check the height of the fundus of the uterus, to see roughly how many weeks' pregnant this lady was. I asked her to lie down, and then gently lifted her nightdress, whilst doing my best to preserve her dignity. I kept thinking that this must be equally embarrassing for her, and that thought helped greatly. We were in this together.

The abdomen in front of me was very large, and I hazarded a guess that the pregnancy must be nearly full term. I then tried to remember what else I had to check for. Which way was the baby lying? Was it head down, or breech? Or was the baby lying transversely? At this point, my fingers were not sure what they were feeling, and I felt the old foe, panic, taking a firm but familiar hold around my throat. My hands had not yet learned how to "read" abdomens, and I felt blind and bemused.

"Well? What can you tell us, Nurse?"

"Um, well, I think that this lady's pregnancy is nearly full term."

"And?"

"And, well, I'm not exactly sure which way the baby is lying." I felt ashamed, but there was no point in pretending that I could feel something that I couldn't.

A theatrically long stare greeted me from above the rims of the spectacles of Mr Woodehouse. "Well," he said at last, "I suppose I had better check this for myself." With that, he expertly palpated Mrs Horrigans's abdomen, and within seconds concluded that the baby was lying in a breech position. I wished that the ground would open up and swallow me. I returned to my orig-

21

inal position next to Abi and followed the entourage, feeling thoroughly dispirited. I'd let the side down.

When Mr Woodehouse finally left the ward, Miss Harrier came across to have a word. "Don't worry about him," she said. "By the time you've been here another few weeks, you'll be able to tell him everything he needs to know." I only hoped that she was right, because as things stood now, I felt as though I knew very little.

The following week, however, things took a definite turn for the better. During our weekly clinical session, we were invited to attend a normal delivery. The mother in question must have been very brave. It was her first baby, and yet she was willing to have eight complete strangers lining the wall at the business end of the room, watching earnestly as she worked so hard to give birth to her child.

Miss Harrier stood with us and explained all that was happening in hushed and respectful tones. Indeed, it was almost like the atmosphere inside a church, where people instinctively become quiet and expectant. Minute by minute, the labour progressed, and after half an hour's pushing and straining by the mother, at last the tip of the baby's head became apparent. We all watched with bated breath. This was a new human being coming into the world. It was a momentous occasion.

Gradually, the head came a little further forward and then, suddenly, incredibly, the entire head became apparent. A minute later, the body followed and there, before our eyes, lay a wet, wriggling, crying child – so beautiful and complete.

I think that we all wanted to applaud – but realised that this would not be very helpful to the baby, so we simply smiled hugely and quietly congratulated the ecstatic mother. As we left the delivery room, we all felt exhausted. Inwardly, we had all been pushing with the mother, trying to will her on. We had also been so impressed by the midwives who had attended her – they knew exactly what to do and when, and it had been a very slick performance.

The atmosphere in the delivery room had reminded me a little of Coronary Care, in that each patient had the undivided attention of the midwife, and that, at any second, the situation could change. Constant vigilance was needed throughout the labour, to ensure that the mother and baby remained in a satisfactory condition. I wondered if I would ever get to grips with all of the assessments and monitoring which was required. On the other hand, I couldn't wait to give it a try.

Chapter Three

It transpired that I didn't have long to wait, because the following week, Abi and I rotated to the Delivery Suite for the first time. In the few hours preceding my first shift I felt sick with nerves. All night I had been plagued by a dream in which I had caused some terrible mishap or other because of my ignorance. It had been so real that the fear remained with me and had a pretty convincing hold as I made my way towards the imposing double doors which led to the Delivery Suite.

I told myself to take a few deep breaths, and to put my shoulders back, and to pretend that I didn't feel quite so useless. A nagging memory kept demanding my attention: "Remember your first day on Coronary Care, and how useless you were then?" I remembered only too well, but recognised that this was now in the past and that it was useless to approach something full of fear.

Fear is a terrible thing. It robs us of our peace and our confidence, and it makes us a slave to bad habits, and a prisoner to the things of the past. The Bible tells us that God's perfect love casts out all fear and, in so doing, releases us from so many chains which hold us back from becoming all that we have been called to be.

"I can do everything through him who gives me strength," I whispered as I swung left into the midwives' office.

There were three midwives already in there. One, a slim, red-haired woman in her twenties, was sitting at the desk, writing up her delivery notes. Behind her stood a tiny oriental woman whose age was difficult to guess, who was busily piling notes onto the desk. The third was a dark-haired woman who was sitting with her back to the door and talking very kindly and reassuringly to a patient on the phone.

She turned and looked around as she finished her call. "Oh, hullo, you must be Hilary. I'm Kate Stainforth. This is Sister Sonia Lim and Staff Midwife Mary Smithers."

"Hello." I hoped that the gulp wasn't audible to everyone in the room.

"Come and put your bag away in one of the lockers in the changing room here," she said. "And then we'll show you around."

The tour of the Suite left me feeling overwhelmed. There was so much equipment which was unfamiliar. Glass-fronted cupboards containing different types of forceps, ventouse extractors, caesarean section and delivery packs. I felt sure that I would never be able to find anything if it was required urgently.

We visited most of the eight delivery rooms, and I was pleased to see that they had all been recently decorated in pretty pastel colours and contained comfortable chairs and bean bags so that the labouring women could be as mobile and comfortable as possible. We went back to the office and took Report from Sister Lim. She gave the impression that she was an extremely knowledgeable and experienced midwife, but her no-nonsense attitude had me quaking in my shoes.

Of the four ladies who were on the Suite, three were in established labour and a fourth was being closely monitored because she had severe pre-eclampsia. This is a condition of pregnancy which causes blood pressure to become dangerously high. It poses a threat to the baby, because the blood supply to the placenta becomes impaired. The high blood pressure could possibly also cause the mother to have a seizure, which would further reduce the oxygen supply to the baby.

As the Report finished, I was allocated the care of one of the ladies whose labour was most advanced. "You work with Mary," Sister Lim barked. "You follow everywhere she goes, and don't get in her way!"

I felt a stab of conscience. Did Sister Lim know about my dream? I pulled myself together and followed meekly behind Mary into room number three.

"Hullo, Susan!" Mary greeted the woman on the delivery bed with warm confidence. Susan looked up from the pillows in which she was burying her head, and managed to grunt a vague "Hi" before rolling around alarmingly on the narrow plinth. Her husband stood at the side, watching his writhing wife with some concern. "I think Sue could do with some pain relief now, she keeps … "

"BLOODY WELL SCREAMING!!!!!" His sentence was completed fortissimo by the writhing figure on the bed. I didn't know whether to giggle or look studious, so I tried a reassuring smile at the husband, and hid behind Mary.

"Sue, I need to examine you to see how far your labour has progressed." I admired the soothing tones of Mary's voice. Did she really feel that calm?

"Ooooooh! Do you have to? I just want to get something for the pain!"

Mary explained that it was essential that we didn't give her strong pain relief too close to the delivery

27

because it could stop her from being able to deliver the baby normally, and it could also depress the baby's breathing severely once it was born. Sue agreed, reluctantly, and her husband valiantly mopped her steaming brow with a cool flannel.

Mary performed a quick internal examination, and as she cleared her trolley, she explained to Sue that she was too late for an injection to help with the pain, but that she could try using Entonox, or "gas and air". Sue nodded desperately from the bed: "Just give me SOMETHING!!!!!"

Mary pointed to the blue-and-white cylinder at the side of the bed. "Give her the mask, Hilary."

I handed Sue the mask, at which point she yelled, "AND WHO THE HELL ARE YOU?"

Her husband looked very sheepish and whispered, "I'm sorry. She's not normally like this."

"I heard that! But I'm not normally in bloody labour, either. It's all your fault, Ian. And if you think I'm ever going to do anything like this again, well, you can bloody think again!"

Ian looked at his fidgeting feet in embarrassment. I could see that he was trying to think of something helpful to say to his wife, but very wisely thought the better of it.

"Oh no! Here comes another one!" The anguished cry was only partially muted by the mask which Sue was clutching to her face for all she was worth.

"Just keep breathing deeply on the mask, Sue, and the gas will soon start to help." Mary was calm and in complete control of the situation. I watched in admiration. The air in the room was then filled with the frantic hissing and pinging of the valve on the Entonox cylinder as Sue sucked in as much pain-relieving gas as she could possibly manage. After about 30 seconds, her breathing slowed and she dropped the mask away from her face, totally relaxed. She grinned drunkenly at Ian.

"This stuff is great!" she said. "It's much better than beer – you should try it!" He looked a little embarrassed, but dutifully carried on wiping his wife's sweaty brow.

Half an hour later I noticed that Sue had started grunting into the mask at the height of each contraction. I looked across the delivery bed at Mary, who seemed to take this sound as a cue to prepare another examination trolley. Mary explained that Sue was probably ready to start the second stage of labour where she could begin to push with her contractions.

Mary quickly and expertly checked how far the baby's head had descended in the pelvis, and then performed an internal examination, during which her face was a picture of concentration. "Right, Sue ... " but Sue was still soporific. "Sue, I want you to stop using the mask now, because it's time for you to have your baby."

Sue's expression changed from one of complete relaxation to sudden panic. "Can't I use this any more? What am I going to do? I can't cope with the pain without it! Get me an injection, or something!"

Mary gently stroked Sue's leg and explained that it was too late for an injection. "Now, Sue, you CAN do this. Your baby is ready to be born now, and it's going to be easier now that you can do something with the pain. Let's sit you up to help you to push."

"Oh no! The pain is coming again! Help! Help!"

"Sue, I need you to take a deep breath now, and to push, push really hard, right down here." Mary patted the mattress with her right hand, her left being held in a vice-like grip by the panic-stricken woman on the bed.

"I can't do this!" Sue shrieked at the top of her

29

voice. It was ear-splitting, and I found myself recoiling. At that moment, there was a sudden gush of liquid as her waters broke. I quickly changed the pad beneath her, and placed several others on the floor because of the sheer volume of liquid which was trickling everywhere.

"Come on, Sue, you can do this!" Mary remained completely focussed on Sue and the fetal monitor. She adjusted the abdominal sensor as the baby descended in the birth canal, and kept a shrewd eye on the readings. She explained that so far, the baby was coping well with the labour, but that it was important that Sue did her best not to prolong things.

The contractions seemed to be coming every other minute, and Mary and Ian held each of Sue's hands and encouraged her to give two long pushes with each contraction. After about 40 minutes, the tip of the baby's head became visible.

"Get me two sterile basins, and open the delivery pack over there, please, Hilary."

I did as I was instructed, and then Mary began to scrub up for the delivery. I was left holding Sue's right hand, and trying not to wince as her nails dug into my arm. She continued to push hard, and the baby's head was being revealed a little more with each contraction.

"Pull the cord, Hilary."

"Which cord?" I asked stupidly. Surely she didn't mean the umbilical cord?

"That red string over there." It was the first hint of annoyance that I had detected in Mary's voice. "I need another midwife to take the baby when he or she is born," Mary explained.

"Oh, yes, of course." I quickly pulled the cord, and could hear a bell ringing outside the room.

"Could you tie up my gown please?" I prised my

hand out of Sue's impressive grasp, and tied the back of Mary's green sterile gown. "Pour out the sterilised solution into both basins, please." There was a new urgency in Mary's voice; we both noticed a sudden progression of the baby's head as Sue continued to grunt and strain.

Within a second, Mary was swabbing Sue with a warm solution and placing sterilised towels underneath her and on her abdomen. She quietly explained everything she was doing to Sue, who was locked into her struggle to push this baby out into the world.

"Is the baby coming out?" she asked slightly bemused.

"Your baby will be out very soon. Just keep pushing down with each contraction, and listen to what I tell you to do, okay?"

"Okay! Here comes another one!"

"Keep going, Susie baby, the baby's nearly here!" In all the busy-ness I had almost forgotten Ian. He was standing now, and cheering his wife on. "Come on! Come on! You can do it! Just a little bit more!"

A few minutes elapsed, but the baby's head remained resolutely in the same place. "Why isn't it coming out?" Sue's voice was pleading now. Mary was looking anxiously at the fetal monitor, and I followed her gaze and noticed that the trace showed the baby's heart rate had dropped to about 80 beats per minute, which was about 60 below normal. The heart rate was no longer recovering between contractions, and this was a sign of fetal distress.

Just then, Sister Stainforth came into the room. "Is everything alright, Mary?"

"We're well into the second stage, but the contractions seem to have slowed slightly and we've just noticed type two dips in the fetal heart rate."

31

"Right, I'll call the senior house officer and the paediatrician." With that, Sister turned and walked briskly out of the room. Sue started another contraction. Mary was meaning business now: "Sue, it's really important that we get this baby out as soon as possible. You MUST push as long and as hard as you can with every contraction. Hilary," she said, turning to me, "give Sue some oxygen, four litres per minute."

I placed the mask over Sue's frightened face, and went back to my position as associate cheerleader. Sue seemed to appreciate the urgency of the situation, and to her credit pushed as long and as hard as she possibly could. Mary kept encouraging her, and after a couple of minutes took hold of her episiotomy scissors and told Sue to pant at the height of the next contraction. During this time, Mary performed a small cut which effectively enlarged the outlet, so that the baby could be born more easily.

With the following contraction, the baby's head was born, and with that, Mary removed and cut the umbilical cord which was tightly entwined around the baby's head. A few moments later, the baby's body slipped on to the green towels on the delivery bed.

Mary wrapped the baby in the towel and rubbed him gently. "It's a boy!" she said. "Congratulations!" With that, the little baby began to snuffle, and then threw back his head and cried. Sister and the senior house officer walked into the room, and relief crossed their faces simultaneously.

Sister immediately took the baby over to the rescusitaire, and the doctor examined him carefully. "He seems fine," said Dr Sandringham. "A lovely bouncing boy."

Sister bundled the baby in some warm towels,

whilst attaching a small plastic clip to the umbilical cord. "Would you like to give him a cuddle, Sue?"

"Would I ever!" Sue reached out for her little boy, all her pain and anguish forgotten in an instant. A moment later, mother, father and little son were huddled together. Nothing else mattered in the whole world.

Mary delivered the placenta, and she and I set about tidying Sue's bed and making her more comfortable before the doctor came to suture her episiotomy. "Well done, Sue. You were fantastic!" I leant forward and gave her a hug. I couldn't believe the miracle that I had just witnessed. Abi was right; midwifery was going to be brilliant.

Chapter Four

The delivery of Sue's baby created an emotional high, and helped greatly as I had to deal with some prejudice from the obstetric senior house officer only a few minutes later. Lucy Deller, the patient with high blood pressure, was causing us serious concern. Mary had asked me to check her observations immediately after leaving Sue's delivery room, and I had found that her blood pressure had increased from 150 over 100, to 180 over 130. I checked it twice, just to make sure.

"Is something wrong?" Lucy asked anxiously.

"Your blood pressure has gone up again, Lucy. I think that we should ask the doctor to have another look at you."

"Okay, but please, whatever you do, please make sure that the baby is alright."

"Of course we will, my love. I'll be back in a few moments. You just ring your buzzer if you feel at all unwell." I handed her the buzzer which had slipped down the back of her bed.

My days in Coronary Care had given me a pretty good ear for auscultating blood pressures, so it came as somewhat of a shock to find my judgement questioned by the doctor who came to assess Lucy a few minutes later.

He checked her B.P. again, and calmly stated that

it was only 140 over 90. The registrar who had been called by Sister looked searchingly at me. "Who said that Mrs Deller's B.P. was so high?"

"I did. I am sure that the reading I obtained was accurate."

The senior house officer smirked. The registrar wrapped the B.P. cuff around Lucy's arm again. "I suppose I'd better check it for myself," he said wearily. I stood hardly daring to breathe as the mercury rose ever higher in the sphygmomanometer. I glanced across at the junior doctor, who was standing confidently with his arms crossed in front of him. After what seemed an age, the registrar removed his stethoscope. He turned to me. "You were right, Nurse. The B.P. is as you said."

I felt a huge relief. I might not yet know my way around the Delivery Suite, or how to cope with obstetric emergencies, but at least I knew how to do *something* properly. The senior house officer raised an eyebrow. "You were just lucky," he mumbled as he walked out of the room.

Sister Stainforth was smiling broadly. One small vindication for the lesser mortals.

I didn't have long to bask in the glory of the moment, because the registrar decided that the time had come to deliver this baby by caesarean section, and Mary and I were given the task of preparing Lucy for theatre. Lucy was understandably distressed. "I want my husband. Please, will someone contact him for me?"

Mary said that she would do this, and I helped Lucy into her theatre gown and catheterised her in readiness for the operation. A few minutes later, we were wheeling Lucy down the corridor to the obstetric theatre, and just as she was about to be anaesthetised, her husband came running down the corridor. "Where is she? Where is Lucy?"

I walked out of the anaesthetic room and spoke with him. "Lucy is just about to be anaesthetised, and your baby will be born very soon."

"Can I see her?"

"I'll just check to see if that is possible."

The anaesthetist gave the thumbs up. "Just for a minute," she said. There followed a tender and intensely emotional minute, and then I was asked to show Martin the waiting room.

"Can I get you a cup of tea?" I asked. He nodded nervously, and I headed for the kitchen. When I returned, he was pacing the floor and looking the colour of a sheet.

About five minutes later, Sister Stainforth came into the room. She was smiling. "Congratulations! Lucy has just given birth to a lovely little girl. We're taking the baby to Special Care to observe her as she is rather small, but you can see her now, if you like."

Martin's face lit up. "Can I really see her? Is Lucy alright?"

"The doctors are just completing the procedure, and she will stay with us post-operatively until her B.P. returns to normal. The operation seems to be going very well."

I led Martin to the post-operative room where one of the midwives was wrapping the tiny baby in several soft blankets. "Here she is." I brought a chair over for Martin to sit on whilst he cuddled his new daughter. His hands were trembling as he reached out to hold her for the first time. A single tear trickled down the young man's face. He looked up with an expression of sheer joy on his face.

"She's so beautiful. I can't believe how lovely she is – all pink and wrinkly." He bent forward and with the most tender of kisses, spoke to his little daughter. "I'm going to make sure that you are the happiest little girl in the whole world. Daddy will always be there for you, no matter what."

It was a remarkably moving scene, and I felt as though I was intruding upon something which was so intimate and special, but at the same time was privileged to be present at the beginning of what hopefully would be a lifetime of loving and caring.

At that moment, I was called away to take a break before the early shift left us alone for the evening. As things stood, there were still three ladies in established labour, and another two had phoned in to say that they were on their way. As I sat down in the staff room, I reflected on the happenings of the past two hours. Two new lives had come into the world, and I felt so privileged to have been involved, albeit in a very minor capacity, with these momentous occasions.

"Time to go back, Hilary." Mary's voice jolted me out of my reverie. We were back in action, and only time would tell exactly what lay ahead.

When we returned to the Suite, I was asked to transfer Sue and her baby to the postnatal ward. She and Ian were still glowing, and neither could take their eyes off their son for more than a second or two. It was as though his birth had flicked a switch inside both of them to instinctively protect him. It was the beginning of the bonding process which would ensure that they would form a powerful attachment to him, and which would carry them through all the trials of parenting that undoubtedly lay ahead.

Sue was soon comfortably settled on the ward, and

I handed the notes to the sister who was on duty. As I returned to the Delivery Suite, I noticed a heavily pregnant woman doubled over in the corridor. Her husband was hanging onto a large holdall and looking around anxiously. Seeing me, he called over, "Can you help, please? My wife is having a baby!"

Oh, Lord, I thought, *what do I do now?* Looking around frantically, I noticed a spare wheelchair and rushed up to the poor woman with it at breakneck speed. "Can you sit down?" I asked, suppressing the thought of lifting her skirt to check if the baby was about to pop out.

"I don't know!" she yelled.

"Come on, get in and I'll wheel you down the corridor. It'll be a lot quicker than walking." Before she could object, I took one of her arms and led her to the wheelchair, then swung her around and seated her in it. I hurriedly placed her feet on the footrests and headed for the delivery rooms as fast as was decently possible. Miss Gibbs's voice from Edinburgh was resurrected in my mind: "Decorum at all cost, Nurses! Decorum at all cost!"

I stopped the wheelchair outside Sister's office, and thankfully, she was there.

"Who is this, Hilary?"

I suddenly realised that I hadn't even asked the woman her name. I looked blankly at Sister. Mr Harding saved the day. "It's Rebecca Harding," he said, adding a little unnecessarily, "and she's having a baby."

Rebecca interrupted with a guttural grunt, "NOW!"

Sister took the hint and wheeled the chair into the only available delivery room. "See if you can find her notes, Hilary!"

"Okay." I rummaged through the notes trolley and

finally found them. When I took them into the room, Rebecca was up on the bed, breathing on the Entonox gas for all she was worth. Sister was performing an internal examination.

"You're ready to start pushing, Rebecca. Let's sit you up to help you push in a better position." I helped her to sit a little higher in the bed, but just as she did this, Rebecca's waters broke, and my shoes were filled with a deluge of warm, straw-coloured fluid.

There was hardly enough time to mop up the floor, before I opened all the relevant delivery packs. Sister didn't bother with a sterile gown; this baby was intent on making a hasty entrance, or exit, whichever way you looked at it.

We didn't have time to attach a fetal monitor as, five minutes later, the air was full of the sound of another crying baby. Another girl – it was amazing! Rebecca's facial expression changed almost instantaneously, from one of complete agony and concentration, to one of sheer joy. It amazed me that the human body and mind could cope with such extremes within such a short time.

I was then sent to help clean the obstetric theatre in preparation for any emergency caesarean sections and, when that was finished, I transferred Rebecca and her new baby to the postnatal ward. Before I knew it, it was seven o'clock and I was sent for my evening break. Returning from this, Mary went through her delivery notes with me and helped me to complete my training manual concerning the observation of normal deliveries. Sister also gave me the relevant information concerning Rebecca's delivery, and then calmly said, "By the time you have witnessed ten, Hilary, we'll be letting you have a go yourself!"

My mind went into a spin – I had already seen two; that meant that I was already a fifth of the way there, and it was only my first day!

The rest of the shift passed much more calmly. All the ladies who had been labouring when we came on duty had now been safely delivered by other midwives, and there was only one more admission: a first-time mum who was in very early labour. By the time we were ready to leave at nine o'clock, I felt as though I had run at least two marathons. So much had happened, and there was so much to learn. The wonderful thing, though, was that it had been an exhilarating eight hours, and I couldn't help feeling that this must be the best job in the world.

Chapter Five

The following day I awoke late in preparation for the first shift of a week of night duty. I didn't feel well and had a very bad headache which just didn't seem to want to go away. As I got up and moved around, I felt as though the floor was lurching uncontrollably, and I felt very nauseous. I was aching all over and felt very weak.

As the day progressed, things didn't seem much better, but I was determined to go to work as I didn't want to miss any experience on Delivery Suite. I arrived there ten minutes early for the nine o'clock shift, and sat down ready to take Report from the evening staff. I was finding it very difficult to concentrate, and the light in the office was making my headache much worse.

"Are you alright, Hilary?" Jayne, one of the midwives on the evening shift, looked across from the desk where she was completing her notes.

"I've just got a bit of a headache, that's all."

"You've not had one too many, have you?" she asked, jokingly. Unfortunately I didn't feel much like joking, so I simply said "No", and left it at that.

Following Report, I was allocated the care of a second-time mum who was in established labour and who had had an uncomplicated pregnancy – the nearest one could guarantee of a promise of a normal delivery. I would normally have felt excited and full of anticipation at the prospect of such a case, but instead I found myself wondering how on earth I was going to cope with the rest of the night.

Clutching my patient's notes, I wandered out of the office and walked smartly into the door frame. "Are you sure you're alright?" It was Sister Drurie who was speaking now. She was my favourite of all the midwives as she embodied complete professionalism with a very human touch.

"I'm sure I'll be alright once I get going, Sister, thank you."

"You look awful. I really think you should go back to bed and see how you are in the morning."

"But how about my lady? I really want to witness another delivery if at all possible."

"Look, Hilary, there'll be plenty more, and to be honest, I don't think that you're fit to take care of anyone in labour. Suppose something happened and you weren't on the ball enough to take care of the situation. We owe it to our patients to give them our best possible care, not to be dragging ourselves around when we're half dead."

Her bluntness made sense, and I reluctantly agreed to return to the Nurses' Home. Sister Drurie said that she would arrange for a doctor from the Occupational Health Department to come across and check me out in the morning, to see how things were then.

I felt too weak to argue and staggered back to the Home, falling gratefully into bed. My head was pounding, and I kept shivering and sweating profusely. It hurt to move my head at all, and I tied a woollen scarf around my head to block out any light. I spent a fretful night where every sound seemed amplified and sent dancing,

44

coloured shapes careering across the blackness of my closed eyes. In spite of painkillers, my head continued to pound in rhythm with my hammering heart.

By morning, I felt so ill that I could hardly manage the short walk to the bathroom without crumpling along the way. At nine o'clock there was a knock at the door. I didn't have the energy to get up to open it for myself, so I simply called, "Come in", in a very small and pathetic voice.

I took off the scarf as the doctor entered the room. She performed a quick assessment and then announced that I would need to be hospitalised. I felt as though things were now becoming farcical. I wasn't supposed to need a hospital – I worked in one, to help other people. I wasn't a patient, but a member of staff – there must be some misunderstanding.

Twenty minutes later an ambulance arrived, and I was driven the 100 metres across the car park to the Casualty Department. The light was agony and I couldn't bear it – I felt as though my head was going to explode. I felt hideously embarrassed to be lying on a trolley, and wondered what on earth I was doing in such a place. I was supposed to be on Maternity, after all.

About half an hour later, a friend from church called Cynthia arrived. Cynthia was a wonderful woman and was the mother of one of the nurses at the hospital. I had only met her a couple of weeks previously when visiting a house church in St Albans. I had been welcomed with open arms and had revelled in the freedom of worship and the faith of the wonderful people there. News of my predicament had spread via the members of the Hospital Christian Fellowship.

I was so pleased to see Cynthia, well, to hear her anyway – one of the nurses had covered my eyes with eye pads and stuck them down to try to keep out the light. Cynthia took hold of my hand and squeezed it reassuringly. I had been at the point of feeling very alone and vulnerable, and her presence was a most timely gift.

"What have you been up to, Hilary?"

"Oh, you know, this and that."

"Was it too many brandies the night before?"

"It must have been," I replied, trying to sound bright, but the effort of trying to laugh sent another dagger-like pulse of pain through my skull.

An hour and a half later, a doctor came to examine me. "I think it's only fair to warn you that you may have viral meningitis, Hilary, and because of your gastric symptoms, we will need to send you to an isolation ward in St Albans."

I didn't know what to say. All I knew was that I felt like death only partially warmed up, and that I needed someone's help to make it through this. Cynthia squeezed my hand. "It's okay, honey, I'll go and get some things from your room, and I'll come with you in the ambulance. My son can come and collect me when you're settled in."

I didn't have the energy to thank Cynthia with more than a grunt and a squeeze of her hand. She was being so kind. Inside me, though, I was rebelling against this ridiculous situation. I was a nurse and had survived Edinburgh with all its strict regimes, so surely a bug wasn't going to defeat me now?

Three hours later, and the trolley was definitely losing some of it charm. All of my joints were complaining violently, and I would have thanked anyone who had the decency to offer decapitation because the pain in my head was so severe. Instead, there followed a bumpy ride along country lanes, swaying around in the back of an ambulance. Each time we went over a pot-hole the driver apologised, which was very decent of him, but I still felt like it had been a journey through hell, all the same.

When we arrived at the hospital, a porter flung open the ambulance doors and pulled down the step at the rear with rather too much enthusiasm. I could hear the driver wincing, "Quietly, please. This lady has a very severe headache." What one had to go through in order to be called a "lady"!

"Sorry, love!" shouted the porter. "Ooops, sorry, love!" he repeated in a whisper.

We trundled along the corridor, and I could feel that the trolley was in a similar state to those found in supermarkets. One of its wheels would intermittently jam, and each time it did, my head wobbled and protested irritably. We eventually came to a halt, and I could hear the porter handing over my notes to the ward sister.

"Right … Hilary, isn't it?"

I smiled as far as my painful face would allow.

"We've got a bed for you in the cubicle over here." I nodded very gently, and found myself being manoeuvred into a small, wooden-floored isolation cubicle. Even the rumbling of the trolley's wheels on the floor made me wince.

I lifted the eye pads so that I could see where I was supposed to slither on to the bed. The porter had offered to lift me across, but I was having none of that. That was for proper patients. I was a nurse and could manage on my own.

I fell back in the bed and couldn't believe how exhausted I felt. My arms and legs felt as though all the strength had been drained from them, and my

47

headache was making me feel very nauseous. I tried to turn over in bed and lie with my face away from the light, but my nightdress was so sodden with sweat that it clung to me like an unwanted sweet wrapper, and prevented me from being able to move.

I lay panting on the bed, wondering what on earth was going on. A moment later, a doctor arrived and announced that she would like to perform a lumbar puncture to confirm the diagnosis. I was in no position to argue, and a few minutes later found myself cuddling my knees whilst she poked a large needle into my spine.

When the procedure was over, I felt completely wretched. I could hear the sounds from the rest of the ward, and everything seemed to be amplified. I could hear every footfall of the nurses as they walked up and down the ward attending to the other patients.

I dozed on and off for what must have been a couple of hours, and my mind was full of brightly coloured images which leapt from one corner of my vision to another. People's faces seemed to appear from nowhere, and to leer, and then fade away. I awoke again, drenched in sweat, and tried to peel my sodden hair away from the back of my neck, but the effort of lifting my head renewed the onslaught of the daggers in my skull. I was completely at the mercy of this thing, and was not enjoying the experience at all.

The evening wore on, and eventually the night staff came on duty. In my experience, night staff fall into two very distinct categories. There are those who are completely devoted to their work and their patients, and there are those who work at night because the pay is better, and if they can get away with not doing very much work, then all the better. I wondered what this group of nurses would be like. I was soon to find out.

Chapter Six

My fitful sleep was rudely interrupted by the light being switched on and the clang of a stainless steel basin as the nurse entered the room.

"Why don't you give yourself a wash?" The tone of the voice was menacing.

"Okay," I said, and tried to turn over towards the sound of her voice.

"You don't need those eye pads on any more, do you?" And before I could answer, I discovered that the decision had been unilateral, and the eye pads were roughly removed. I gasped involuntarily at the brightness of the light. "Where's your soap bag?"

"I'm not sure. I think it's been put in the locker."

"Ah yes, here it is. Right, I'll leave you to it then." And with that, she turned and left the room. I fumbled in the soap bag in search of the flannel, and was gasping with the effort of keeping my head slightly raised from the pillow. I found the flannel and dipped it in the tepid water, but found that I had no strength to wring it out. I had to keep stopping every few seconds as I sloshed the soggy cloth around my face and tried to wipe the back of my neck, which was saturated with sweat. What on earth was happening to me?

I toyed with the idea of changing the nightdress, but gave up when I realised that it too was in the locker,

49

which was way out of my reach. A minute later, the nurse returned and whisked the basin away. I looked at her large, lumbering form with some resentment as she poured the water away.

My mouth felt like a sandpit and I would have welcomed the opportunity to rinse it, but that, apparently, was not part of the service. I was beginning to wonder where nurses like this came from. I felt humiliated and powerless, and this woman seemed to be relishing the power she exercised as she withheld appropriate care from her patient.

She slammed the basin down in the cupboard under the sink, then turned on her squeaky heels and marched out of the room, flicking the light switch off as she went. I supposed that I should be grateful for small mercies.

I tried to pray, but had no energy left. I hoped that God would understand that I needed Him more than ever now, even though it was impossible to put my heart's cry into words.

The night hours passed fitfully as I was constantly disturbed by the sounds on the ward. The pain in my head seemed to have exaggerated my sense of hearing, and I could hear every word that was spoken at the nurses' station. At two o'clock the staff were sitting eating toast and drinking tea and the nurses began to discuss each of the patients in turn. I was horrified to hear some of the comments which were made about my fellow inmates. Then I recognized my nurse's voice, and was more than horrified. "I think she's just putting it on – she's not ill at all, well, not physically, anyway."

"What do you mean, Denise?"

"Well, you know, some people pretend to be ill so that they can get the doctors to perform lots of tests and operations and the like. What's it called again?"

Another voice, male this time, answered. "You mean Munchausen's syndrome?"

"That's it. I think that's her problem, silly bitch!"

There was a multiple giggle, but their further comments were drowned out from my ears by the thudding of my very indignant heart. What was I to do now? I couldn't get up and walk out of the ward, which was my preferred option, so I would have to wait until the following afternoon at visiting time until Cynthia came. How could anyone stay in a place like this? I was totally dependent upon these people to help me, but they, instead, were using the opportunity to take a dig at one of their own. Not for the first time, I felt ashamed of some of the members of my profession.

The night did eventually pass, and with the dawn came the coughing of the birds in the surrounding trees, and a cold realisation that, one way or another, I was going to have to get out of here. The morning shift arrived, but I didn't feel that I could voice my complaint about the previous night's unprofessional conduct to anyone whilst I was so alone, and unable to defend myself. I simply became a totally compliant patient, asking for nothing and willing the hours to pass until the afternoon.

I wondered how many patients had suffered silently like this? The doctors came around and peered into each of the cubicles. I simply pretended to be asleep and kept my face towards the wall. "We're still awaiting the results of the lumbar puncture, but her temperature is still very high." It's great how we can become a collection of symptoms. There was the shuffling of many feet, and the entourage swayed quietly along, ready to take a squint at the unfortunate inmate next door.

Lunchtime came and went, but I still couldn't face any food. Water was just about staying down, but the effort of lifting my head to drink it was almost too costly. Eventually, Cynthia and her son Richard and his wife Deb arrived. As soon as I heard their voices, tears of relief began to flow.

"What's the matter, Hil?" It was Richard's unmistakable voice.

"I'm really pleased to see you, that's all. I'm sorry, I didn't mean to cry." I grabbed a tissue and tried to blow my nose, but the sound felt like a herd of elephants on a stampede in my brain. I resorted to dabbing, instead.

"What's been going on? You look terrible."

"Thanks."

"Has something happened?"

"Well, in a way, I suppose it has."

"What?" All three voices chorused together.

I was too exhausted to beat about the bush, so I described the incident of the previous night. Richard and Deb were indignant. "How dare they say such a thing? This is totally unprofessional. Right!" Richard stood up hastily. "I'm going to have a word with Sister. You're not going to stay in this place one moment longer."

I didn't want to cause a scene, but it seemed that it was now out of my control. "Please, Richard, don't make a fuss..." But he was already halfway through the doorway. Cynthia and Deb were tidying the locker, and putting away some grapes and tissues which they had thoughtfully brought with them.

A minute later, Richard returned with Sister. "What is this I hear happened during the night, Hilary?"

I looked despairingly at Richard. "Go on," he said. "Tell Sister everything that happened."

I finished the tale with the explanation that I wasn't trying to cause trouble, but wanted to make clear that the situation had been, and still was, extremely upsetting.

"I see," said Sister.

"Well, Hilary can't stay here if the staff are going to treat her like this, can she?" Richard was good at getting to the point.

"I will see if there is another bed on one of the medical wards. Will that be okay?" Sister looked at Richard and he was nodding his agreement.

"I'd rather go home, if you don't mind," I said.

"You can't even sit up at the moment, so I'm afraid that discharge home is completely out of the question. Leave it with me and I will see what I can do." Sister turned and left us. She was trying to be helpful, and was strangely unsurprised by the situation. I wondered how many times this had happened in the past?

Half an hour later my visitors were quietly drinking tea and talking about people at church and the world in general. I was dozing on and off and was startled by Sister's return. "I've found a bed for you on the Medical Wing, and I've arranged an ambulance to take you there. It will be here in about an hour, is that okay?"

"That's fine, Sister, thank you." I was doing my best to be polite.

When the porters arrived, there was a repeat performance of the previous day, trying to move from the bed onto the trolley. It was an ungainly performance by anyone's standards, and by the time it was accomplished, the exertion had left me totally exhausted, once again.

It's funny how news travels in a hospital. If a patient develops a reputation for being "difficult", then the staff put on this "Don't mess with me" expression. I could see this on the faces of the porters now. The trolley was wheeled roughly around the bends in the corridor, and the doors were slammed shut on the ambulance with unnecessary force. I winced and tried not to cry out as the reverberating sound surged and rattled through my brain. When would this all end?

A short drive, at speed, over the humps which were supposed to slow the traffic down, and we were then trundling along another twisting corridor, up in a lift, with the bright ceiling lights boring down upon us, and then through the ward doors, which were allowed to crash against the trolley next to my head. I was getting the message, loud and clear.

To my surprise, I was wheeled into a single room and deposited on the bed. The porters let the trolley crash into the door on their way out, just for good measure. I lay trembling on the bed, and pulled the thin bedclothes around me for protection. The lights were unbearably bright in this room, and I was just trying to find a position where they weren't shining directly into my eyes when a voice spoke to me from the doorway. "I hear you didn't like the service down in the isolation ward?" There was an unmistakable note of jeering in the voice. Not again, surely.

"It was a very unpleasant experience," I replied, and left the nurse to draw her own conclusions.

The evening wore on and, as the darkness fell, I began to feel a little better. The evening shift went home and the night staff were doing their observations and settling everyone down for the night. I fell into a troubled sleep. My dreams were full of brightly coloured shapes and hideous faces merging and swirling before my befuddled eyes. Suddenly, I awoke with a start. Someone was tapping my arm.

I opened my eyes painfully, and from the light in the main ward I could see the enormous silhouette of a figure wearing a starched cap. My mind raced back to the nights on duty in Edinburgh, when the nursing officers would pounce, unannounced, from the gloom. It was happening again.

"Miss McIntosh?" The voice sounded cold and hard. "Don't even think about making an official complaint."

With that, the huge figure turned and left the room, shutting the door, and I was left, staring into the dark night.

Chapter Seven

Five days later I was able to be discharged from the hospital, and Cynthia kindly offered to let me stay with her.

Cynthia's home was warm and comfortable, and it was lovely to be out of the hospital environment. More than anything, I appreciated the peace and quiet, and each day, I was hopeful that I would be able to think about returning to work. But the days rolled into weeks, and I found that it was still impossible to tolerate the light, or to sit up for very long. The pain in my head was excruciating, and the fatigue overwhelming. Cynthia and Richard were becoming anxious, and decided to call out a general practitioner for a home visit.

When the doctor arrived, he walked into my darkened bedroom, and heaving open the curtains, declared, "There is no need for all of this. I'll give you some valium – you are obviously depressed – and then, get on with your life." He scribbled out the prescription and without another word, turned and left the room.

Once again I found myself shell-shocked in a horizontal position. I wasn't depressed. I loved my job, and I had good friends who were willing to help me. I was also a very determined person, and resented the implication to the contrary. The frustrating thing was that I just couldn't get up and "get on with my life", and that was the whole problem.

The weeks passed, and gradually the months went by. I mourned the loss of my midwifery experience, and constantly wondered how Abi and the rest of my class were getting on. Outside, the seasons changed and I watched the leaves tumbling during the first storms of the autumn. What on earth was I going to do now?

Cynthia and Richard decided that they would invite a friend from a neighbouring Pentecostal church over to pray for me. The man in question was larger than life in practically every sense of the word. Lars had moved to Britain from Sweden a few months previously because he felt that the Lord had called him over to learn more about church leadership.

On the evening in question, he burst into Cynthia's living room with tremendous energy and vitality. He sat down on the edge of his seat and proceeded to tell me that God was going to heal me. "I believe that anything is possible with God," he said. "Indeed, I believe that one day, I will be able to walk on water, just like Jesus did."

Bully for you, I thought, *but how about my head?*

Cynthia, Richard and Lars began to pray, and I sat on the settee with my eyes shut, praying quietly that God would help me. I felt as though everything was hopelessly out of control. Lars, becoming more fervent in prayer, laid his hands on my head and commanded the pain to go, in the Name of Jesus.

I don't know exactly what I expected to happen, but nothing did, so I continued just to sit there with my eyes closed, hoping for the best. After a further few minutes, Lars told me to open my eyes, which I did, only to find that the brightness of the living room light had its usual painful effect.

"How do you feel?" Lars was beaming confidently at me.

"I ... I feel just the same," I replied.

"God will heal you. Walk by faith and not by sight."

Great, I thought.

With that, Lars rose to leave. Just before he left the room he paused in the doorway. "I'm going to get married soon."

Cynthia smiled politely and asked, "Oh, that's lovely. When and to who?"

He looked searchingly at me, and for an awful minute I thought that I might just be on the receiving end of a double whammy, but he turned back to Cynthia and said, "I haven't met her yet, but I'll know when I do." I wondered if the girl in question would share in the secret, or just have her fate announced when it seemed right to Lars.

He left the room with the same characteristic energy and confidence, his long blond hair billowing behind him as he lowered his head to pass through the doorway. I sighed with relief. All I knew was this: his prospective bride would have to be a woman not only of great faith, but also great stamina, if she was going to stand a chance of keeping up with him.

My own faith was hanging in there, but the energy side was definitely the weakest link in the equation, so I excused myself from Cynthia and Richard and proceeded to crawl upstairs to bed.

The following morning, I awoke tentatively to hope that a miraculous healing might have taken place overnight. With great disappointment I found that things were just the same. Perhaps it was my lack of faith? Maybe I didn't really want to get better? I shuddered at the very thought, and hung on grimly to what I knew to be the truth.

Cynthia and Richard were also very hopeful that things would improve, and I felt embarrassed and ashamed to admit that nothing had changed. I tried to push myself to do more, but the end result was always the same – I was left completely exhausted and unable to move.

The weeks rolled on, and I felt desperate and alone. I knew that I was becoming a source of great concern for Cynthia and her family and this was the last thing that I had intended. Why wouldn't this thing go away? It was supposed to.

I was sent to the Royal Free Hospital in London for a brain scan, and this really worried me. Supposing it was a brain tumour? I was examined by a doctor there and made to perform various activities whilst he and a colleague looked on with perplexed expressions on their faces. I hated this, and returned home exhausted, demoralised and none the wiser.

Miss Harrier telephoned to see how things were progressing. I tried to sound as positive as possible, but felt very ashamed to have been away from work for so long.

"There is another intake of student midwives in February, if you would be interested?"

"Can I think about it, please?"

"Yes, of course. Just let me know when you have made up your mind."

My mind was anything but made up. Over the weeks, I had been toying with the idea of trying to return to Edinburgh. At least I was known there as a hard worker and not a malingerer. Perhaps this was what the Lord intended? The continuing indecision created a vicious circle of doubt which made decision-making even more difficult. I found myself one morning, sitting on a chair and wondering if it was possible just to dismiss your spirit, like Jesus did when He died. I gave it a try, but it just wasn't taking any notice, and like the rest of me, wasn't going anywhere at all.

I decided that I would try to make plans to return to Edinburgh, and telephoned the Royal Infirmary to ask about midwifery training there instead. The call was answered by a lovely woman who checked my records, and said that they would be delighted to include me in their list of new students. That was it, then. The way seemed open to return. I contacted Miss Harrier to let her know of my decision.

"But you can't go, Hilary. With you we have eight students for the next course. If you don't join the group then the course will have to be postponed until an eighth person can be found. You really must honour our agreement."

I put the receiver down with my mind in turmoil. I didn't want to stay down south any longer. I wanted to go back to my nursing friends and to all that was familiar in Edinburgh. I tried to pray but nothing seemed to be getting through, so I pulled out my Bible, and read the notes for that morning.

The words "Those who honour me I will honour" jumped out of the page. What was it that Miss Harrier had said? "You must honour your agreement, Hilary." Was God trying to tell me something? I mulled it over, and the more I prayed, the more peaceful I felt about staying in Welwyn Garden City. Looking at the situation logically, it was not very rational to stay, because life had definitely been extremely difficult for the past five or six months, but it was as though God was saying that I should honour Him by honouring the midwifery college which had kept a place open for me.

I called Miss Harrier once again, and she was very gracious about the entire episode, so plans were made for me to begin training from the beginning in four weeks' time. All I needed now was a miracle.

Chapter Eight

With each passing day my strength gradually returned. It was a slow process and some days were better than others. As the start date for resuming the course drew nearer, I found myself panicking and wondering if I would ever remember all those hormones again.

I had to believe that the Lord wanted me to do this all again, and that if this was His plan, then He would have to supply all the mental and physical strength needed for each day. It was a journey of faith. I could no longer simply follow my own feelings, but had to trust that the Lord was going to carry me through the training. If I was obedient and kept to my part of the deal, then I knew that He would do the rest.

Throughout all of this, Cynthia, Richard and Deb had been wonderfully supportive. I thanked the Lord every day for them and saw them as part of His wonderful provision. I was reminded of how God had provided for all the needs of the tribes of Israel as they spent 40 years wandering in the desert, totally dependent upon Him for everything. The Bible story tells us how He supplied food, "manna", a type of bread or biscuit, every morning in just the right quantities to sustain His people. It seemed as though the more reliant people were on God, the more perfect and precious were His gifts. I was beginning to learn how important it was to trust and honour Him in all things.

Cynthia said that she was happy for me to stay with her even though I was now back at work, and I decided that the time had come to buy a car. This would make getting to work much easier, and I would also be able to transport Cynthia to the shops and to church whenever she needed help. I looked in the local newspaper under the Cars for Sale section, and my eyes were immediately drawn to a small advertisement which read: "Mini for sale. £200, or near offer." I prayed over the advertisements, "Lord, if this is the right car, please show me."

Nothing happened, so I thought I should once again return to the Bible. I didn't expect to receive direct advice about purchasing a car, but knew that God was able to speak powerfully through His Word. I was reading from the Psalms at the time and a verse leapt out of the page at me: "He makes the clouds his chariot."

It seemed that God was confirming my need for a chariot, too. I fell about laughing, amazed by God's goodness, and the fact that He cared about whether I had a car or not.

Richard agreed to come and check the car with me. It turned out to be a very old, dark blue Mini. Inside, its indicator stick had a flashing light on the end, and the full-beam switch was situated on the floor, to the left of the clutch pedal. When we took it for a test drive, it sounded as though there was a crate of pigeons in the back. But it was lovely, and I had a tremendous sense that this was the right car for me.

Handing over the cash, I proudly sat in the driving seat, and drove tentatively away. There were a few things I needed to learn about driving in Welwyn, and it proved to be a steep learning curve. In Edinburgh, where I had passed my test, there weren't any round-abouts on my training route, so it was perplexing to find that there were dozens, of varying sizes, here in Welwyn Garden City.

Richard sat in the passenger seat, white knuckles clutching either side of his seat, and with the colour completely drained from his face. I did manage to give way to the traffic coming from the right, but didn't negotiate the centre of the roundabout very well, and at one point we found ourselves virtually on two wheels, instead of four.

Richard grinned fixedly, which was very much to his credit. "That's fine, Hilary. But perhaps, next time, you could steer round the island, just a little bit more?" We returned home both realising that perhaps a little more practice wouldn't go amiss, but Richard seemed quite happy that I should acquire that on my own.

Back at the hospital, I was assigned to the postna-tal ward and was loving every minute of it. I enjoyed the combination of practical advice and parentcraft educa-tion which went on there, together with the nursing care. It was a very rewarding and satisfying place in which to work. I appreciated my work more than ever and wanted to make up for the previous six months when my career had been in ruins.

The weekly rounds with Mr Woodehouse contin-ued, and he unfailingly asked me to perform examina-tions on the antenatal ladies in front of the entourage. Each week, my fellow students could be sure that they were safe from his prying eyes – it seemed that I was the only one chosen for this weekly dose of public humiliation.

One morning, we all followed Mr Woodehouse

into a side room, and within seconds, his gnarled index finger was once again pointing straight at me. "You, Nurse, you come and examine this lady and tell me what you can feel."

My fellow students all smiled reassuringly at me. That was nice of them, but I wished that this experience could be shared by them, too. I rubbed my hands briefly to warm them.

"Hullo," I said to the lady in the bed. "I'm just going to check which way your baby is lying, is that alright?"

Linda nodded obligingly, and lifted up her night-dress. Her abdomen looked an odd sort of shape. Now pregnant abdomens do come in all shapes and sizes, depending upon which way the baby is lying, but this one seemed to be all over the place.

I placed my left hand at the top of the uterus, and thought to myself that she seemed to be the right size for a full-term pregnancy. I then ran both hands down either side of the abdomen, feeling for the smooth contour of a baby's back. I couldn't feel one, on either side. What I could feel, however, was kicking feet, on both sides. Now, either this baby was doing the splits, or there was more than one in there.

I quickly palpated around and found one head low down on Linda's left side, and one higher up on her right. Bingo! I think Mr Woodehouse saw the light bulb go on, because at that precise moment he asked, "Well, Nurse, tell us what you have found."

I was just about to triumphantly reveal my findings when he said, "No, on second thoughts, you there, medical student. You have a feel and see what you can find."

I couldn't believe it. Somebody else was in the hot seat for a change. I tried not to look too smug, but

66

smiled at Miss Harrier, who winked back. The medical student, however, was busily pummelling Linda's abdomen as though it were a large dough ball.

"Well?" Mr Woodehouse looked enquiringly at the alarmed features on the young man's face. The Pinard stethoscope which was used to auscultate the fetal heart was shaking visibly in his hand. I felt very sorry for him. Medical students only spent a short time learning the basics of obstetrics, and consequently had very little practical experience. It seemed very unfair that he should be put in this humiliating position.

"Well?" Mr Woodehouse was beginning to sound impatient. The medical student began to explain that Linda's abdomen was the correct size for a full-term pregnancy, and that he thought that the baby was lying head down in the pelvis, with its back on Linda's right side.

Miss Harrier looked searchingly at me, and for an awful moment I thought that I must have been completely wrong in my assessment. The brief, glorious moment of confidence seemed to evaporate more quickly than it had arrived.

"What did you find, Nurse?"

The heat was on again. I cleared my throat, and prayed that I would remember what I had felt. I moved back to Linda's side and talked Mr Woodehouse through my findings. When I had finished, I could feel the blush rising faster than a cuttle fish could change colour. I gulped nervously whilst I awaited Mr Woodehouse's verdict.

"Let me have a feel," he murmured as he pushed past me and performed his palpation single-handedly – a manoeuvre for which he was famous. There was a long theatrical pause whilst he looked from the medical

67

student to me and back again. I could see the smiles on the faces of all the entourage. This was an entertaining spectacle for them. I looked imploringly at Linda's abdomen.

"Well done, Nurse," he said finally. "That was a difficult one. There are indeed two fetuses in there, and they are lying in such a way that they are not very easy to find."

The relief was enormous and there were broad smiles on all the midwives' faces. There was a corresponding grimace from the medical fraternity. I just felt hugely relieved that perhaps I was learning something after all.

After the round we returned to the school of midwifery to continue with a study day which concluded with a written exam. This was the pattern each week, and it meant that we had to keep up with our theoretical studies whilst working full time on the wards. The busy-ness meant that time passed very quickly, and before long, we were sitting an exam which would determine whether we would be allowed to continue training. Thankfully we all passed, and we continued with our rotations through antenatal clinic and ward, to Delivery Suite, theatre and postnatal ward.

My favourite secondment, however, was to the community, to work with a midwife there for three weeks. I was sent to work just outside Harlow, and my little blue Mini and I travelled around with Viv, as she showed me her "patch".

Viv was a very kind and lovely woman, in her late forties, with two children who were studying at university. She ran several antenatal clinics from a doctors' surgery, including parentcraft classes for prospective parents. She also delivered as many of her "ladies" as possible at the local general practitioner's unit, and then cared for them postnatally in their own homes. In spite of being extremely busy, Viv always gave the impression that she had plenty of time for everyone, and it was a great privilege to work with her.

On the final week of the secondment, Viv asked me to give a parentcraft talk to the antenatal ladies on the subject of labour. This topic was considered the "Big One", as the one thing that is very prominent in the minds of expectant mums is the issue of how the baby is going to come into the world, and how much it is going to hurt.

I spent hours preparing the talk, and made posters and copious notes concerning the various types of analgesia on offer, and the benefits or drawbacks of each. I borrowed a doll and model pelvis to demonstrate the baby's movements during the second stage of labour, and turned up at the antenatal clinic with them tucked under my arm.

Viv introduced me to her ladies and, as I stood up to speak, my knees started knocking. I had to swallow hard as my leaping heart threatened to completely constrict my tight throat. I kept thinking of Miss Gibbs and her "decorum", and came to the conclusion that public speaking involves a lot of acting, and that I wasn't very sure that this was something that I was any good at. *Help, Lord.* I uttered a silent prayer and then began to speak.

I finally came to the end, and was encouraged to see that the ladies were still watching attentively and had a lot of questions which I did my best to answer. As we left the clinic, Viv was very encouraging, and I felt very relieved as we drove away from the clinic. Viv turned the car towards the suburbs and we prepared for some home visits and postnatal checks.

We arrived at a huge white house with pillars on either side of the front door. Viv looked across and smiled. "They're a lovely couple in here ... You're not frightened of dogs, are you?" she added as an after-thought. I shook my head. I would just hide behind Viv – she would know what to do.

We rang the doorbell, and a few moments later, there was the sound of several dogs barking. It wasn't the sound of your average yappy hound, but rather the sound of a pack of dogs which accompanies a hunt. I grinned nervously at Viv, who seemed completely unruffled by the hellish din.

The door was eventually opened by a very tired-looking young man. "Oh, hullo," he said. "He's had us up all night. I'm sorry that we're not very organised today."

"That's alright," said Viv. "When a new baby comes, the housework goes."

We were ushered into a huge hallway. "Don't worry about the dogs," he said. At that moment three striped Great Danes strode up to us. One of them began sniffing at my bag. I resisted the temptation to raise my black bag out of its reach. If it had stood on its hind legs, it would have been able to reach the bag anyway. Viv and I stood perfectly still, and very slowly, the three dogs began to circle us, looking at us very suspiciously. This continued for several minutes and was accompanied by an unearthly growling from the three animals. I was beginning to think that we might just become a small snack for the dogs if the mother of the baby took much longer.

With each circuit, the dogs seemed to be getting

closer to us, and the growling became louder. "Nice doggie" didn't seem to suit the situation, somehow.

The growling was interrupted by the mother, at last. "Stop that, you three!" The dogs slunk off towards the kitchen, and Viv and I were able to move at last. We followed Jenny into her spacious living room, and proceeded to check baby Ben, who now weighed a very respectable nine pounds.

We then went upstairs to perform Jenny's postnatal checks, and were led into a beautiful bedroom, with an en suite bathroom, gold taps included. Those taps reminded me of the opulence I had known in Hong Kong, and I wondered how it was that some people had so much, and yet others had so little.

This thought was graphically illustrated by our next visit. As we left the exquisite white house, Viv drove back towards the town, onto one of the council estates. As we walked down the garden path, we could see that the paint on the door was peeling badly, and the window frames looked rotten. There was smearing on the inside of the downstairs windows, which looked as though it had been made by a multitude of sticky little fingers.

It came as no surprise when the door was opened by an exhausted mother, who was shouting at her two-year-old son to "Stop it, before I kick yer 'ead in!" The odour of the house was appalling – it was an unmistakable mixture of damp, urine and tobacco. "Come in," said the mother, "and sit down."

I looked enquiringly at Viv – should we sit down in this place, or would it be better to remain standing? Viv, unruffled as ever, accepted the woman's hospitality and sat down on the settee. I sat next to her and controlled the urge to retch, as the smell of urine was very much worse down there.

"Would yer like a drink?"

I really felt that I needed to draw the line some-where. "No, thank you very much, but I'm fine." Viv said the same, and we carried on with the postnatal checks on mother and baby. The baby was a little girl who already had a dummy rammed in her mouth to keep her quiet, although she was only four days old. She looked small and unhappy, and Viv questioned the mother about feeding.

"Oh, she always finishes her bottle. She's good at that, but she does keep crying."

"How often are you feeding her?" asked Viv.

"Every five or six hours."

"And how much does she take at a feed?"

"A couple of ounces." This meant that the baby was only getting about ten ounces of milk at best in every 24 hours – about half of what she needed. Viv was about to say this when the mother added, "I've already started to put tea in 'er bottle – seems to like it."

I tried not to look too horrified. The tannin in tea is very harmful to a developing brain, and should never be given to babies of any age, let alone one who is only four days old.

Viv weighed the little girl and found, unsurpris-ingly, that she had lost a little more weight since she was born. She went on to advise the mother that the feeds needed to be at least twice as often, and that if the baby was finishing every bottle, it probably meant that she needed to increase the quantity of milk in the bottle further still.

I looked across the room at the little boy who was beating hell out of a small plastic chair with a toy ham-mer. I wondered how much of a chance his little sister would stand in a place like this. His mother tried in vain to keep him quiet, but he just wasn't listening. I hoped that she had someone who could help her, because with the two children, she really had her hands full.

Viv performed the postnatal checks on the mother, and advised her that it was really important that she did not smoke in the same room as the baby. She tried to encourage the mother to attend a local mother-and-baby club which was running at the local church, and she gave the mother her telephone number and that of a health visitor, in case she needed any help before Viv's next visit, the following day.

As we left the house, Viv turned to me and smiled. "From the sublime to the ridiculous, eh?"

I nodded sadly. "I wish that we could do something to help people in these difficult situations. It makes you feel so helpless, doesn't it?"

"We can't live other people's lives for them, you know. We all have to make choices. All we can do is to try to help people make the best of what they have." What wise words.

Chapter Nine

The community placement came to an end all too quickly, and I returned to the hospital with renewed respect for all postmen, who daily face the canine friends of the British population.

I was looking forward to the next rotation to the Delivery Suite with a mixture of excitement and nervousness. There was still so much to learn, and I always felt that ladies in labour were something of a "ticking bomb" – anything could go wrong at any time, and it was up to the midwives to ensure that it didn't.

The babies themselves were not always born knowing how to breathe adequately, either, and this was another area which was of great concern to me. It seemed as though a midwife had to have a sixth sense, almost, about the baby during the delivery, as the monitors did not always tell the full story. Sometimes the trace depicting the baby's heart rate would look alarming, with large decelerations during and after a contraction, and yet the baby would be born crying lustily. At another time, the trace would not look too bad, but the baby was born looking very flat, and took a lot of persuasion to take its first breath.

Watching the experienced midwives at work, and dealing with more and more deliveries myself, I gradually began to become attuned to the nuances of labour, and gained in confidence in dealing with babies who needed some help to readjust to life outside the womb.

One evening shift, however, my confidence in our ability to bring babies safely through the birth process took a definite knock. We were exceptionally busy, and one of the sisters from the Special Care Baby Unit had been brought down to the Delivery Suite to help, because we seemed to be in the middle of a mini baby boom.

In one of the rooms, a mother was in established labour, and she was expecting twins. I had hoped that I would be able to witness the delivery, but I was told that I was needed in an adjacent room, where a mother was expecting her third child.

My patient, who had had two perfectly normal deliveries previously, seemed to be progressing well. She was coping with only Entonox for pain relief, and was walking around, keeping as mobile as possible. Suddenly, however, there were signs that the baby was getting distressed. The fetal heart monitor showed a continuing depression in rate, and Wendy, the midwife in charge, suggested that we perform an internal examination to assess Janine's progress. I examined her and found that she was almost fully dilated, at nine centimetres.

"Pop the membranes, Hilary," instructed Wendy. As I did so, the fluid which drained away was greenish in colour, a sure sign of fetal distress. Wendy put on some gloves and examined Janine quickly. "Call the senior house officer and the paediatrician!"

I left the room fast and my hands were shaking as I lifted the receiver to bleep the relevant doctors. I waited for an agonising minute for the call to be answered by the switchboard operator. Half a minute later and both doctors had responded and said that they were on their way. As I walked back into the delivery room, Wendy was explaining to the parents that a forceps delivery was looking very likely. Janine was lying on her left side and had an oxygen mask over her face. She was looking pale, tired and frightened.

"Set up a forceps trolley, Hilary!"

I sped around the room, filling the stainless steel basins with sterile lotions and opening all the relevant packs as quickly as possible. Doctor Brahms arrived, and took one look at the fetal heart trace.

"Right," she said. "We are going to help you deliver this baby as quickly as possible, Janine." Turning to me she said, "Put her legs up in the stirrups, please. And be quick about it!"

I did as I was instructed, and Janine began to bear down with each contraction. The room was silent apart from the sound of the fetal heart monitor which slowed dramatically with each contraction and seemed to take an eternity to return to a more normal rate. Wendy was looking worried. "I think the baby is stuck in the transverse and is unable to rotate its head through the birth canal."

I knew that this was a bad sign, because if the head did not rotate slightly then it could not progress any further down the birth canal. A much more invasive procedure would be required to deliver the baby.

"Call the anaesthetist!" Dr Brahms's face was a picture of concern and concentration. As I rushed to the office once again, I was praying silently for the mother and baby struggling in the room behind me.

Within a couple of minutes the anaesthetist arrived and was preparing to perform a pudendal block, which anaesthetises the area surrounding the cervix and lower birth canal. My hands were still shaking as I drew up the local anaesthetic into the large syringe. I kept praying urgently as the doctor quickly administered the drugs, and within a few moments was applying the large Keillands rotation forceps. The room was rigid with tension – everyone was urging Janine to continue with her efforts, and a trickle of sweat ran unheeded down the side of Dr Brahms's pale face. The fetal heart monitor continued to fill the room with a slow beep, and Janine groaned as the forceps began to turn inside her. Her face was pale and drawn, and her husband's eyes seemed sunken and held the expression of desperation.

And then, a few seconds later, the baby emerged. He was purple, and had a huge amount of moulding which was distorting the true shape of his head. As he flopped into the waiting arms of the paediatrician, we could see that although he was a little the worse for wear, he was alive and making valiant attempts to breathe for himself. He looked like a miniature boxer who has been knocked out several times during a fight, and doesn't know when to quit.

The baby gurgled and spluttered as he was placed on the rescusitaire, and then, to everyone's immense relief, he began to cry, announcing to the world that he had arrived and that he had survived his ordeal. As he cried, it was as though a huge wave of relief came over us all. In my heart, I was praising God for His mercy, and thanking Him for the gift of this precious person. Janine and her husband were both crying and hugging each other, and Wendy was preparing the suture trolley, a huge grin on her face.

I took the used trolleys to the sluice and was preparing to clear away all the debris. I suddenly felt very tired, and quite emotional. We had come very close to losing this little baby, and that thought shocked me deeply. As I walked through the sluice doors, however, I was in for another surprise.

In all the busy-ness, I had completely forgotten the dramas of the twin delivery which had been taking place in the next room. I pushed my trolley up to the sink area in preparation for cleaning the instruments. There was a delivery tray wrapped in green towels and placed on the draining area. As I walked past, a small object caught my attention from the corner of my eye. As I turned to look at it properly, my heart missed a couple of beats. There, hanging limply, was a tiny human hand – it was one of the twins.

I stopped in my tracks and stared, transfixed by what I saw. Sadness mingled with horror and nausea flooded over me. I had begun to think that we could always ensure a happy outcome with all of our technology and experience, and yet, here lay a tiny person who had never had the chance to live at all.

In spite of my revulsion, I felt compelled to look at the baby more closely. I lifted the green towel slightly, and saw a chubby little arm, which led up to the shoulder. The baby's head was turned away from me, and I didn't feel that I could look any more. I gently covered the little body once again, and cleared my own trolley, washing the instruments quickly. As I did so, my eyes kept wandering to the little body, and I felt the old fear of death creeping up my spine once again.

When I had finished in the sluice, I put on a smile, and walked back into Janine's room. She was happily cuddling her new son, and she and her husband were discussing names for him.

The scene in the adjacent room could not have been more different. As I walked into the sluice area once again to dispose of the green towels, I could see through the window in the door that on the delivery bed lay a pale young woman who looked completely shell-shocked. Her face was stained with tears, and I could hear her crying.

Her husband sat by her side, and his young face struggled to contain his own emotions. On the resuscitation trolley lay the remaining twin, and the paediatrician and the sister from Special Care were working quickly to try to stabilise her condition. There was an eerie quietness about the room, as though every occupant was willing the little baby to make some noise, some effort to breathe for herself. In such circumstances time seems to stand still, and everyone becomes aware of their own breathing, wishing that they could impart their own breath to the little child lying limply before their anxious eyes.

Minutes passed, and I stood praying fervently that the Lord would touch this little child, and her parents, and bring hope out of what had already been too much of a tragedy. I watched as the paediatrician expertly inserted a tiny endotracheal tube into the baby's throat, and connected the tube to a miniature bag which was used to inflate the lungs with air. The baby's chest began to rise and fall with each squeeze of the bag, and her colour began to improve.

The doctor checked the baby's heart rate again and, satisfied that the baby was now fit for transfer to Special Care, he turned to the parents, said a few words, and then took the baby away in an incubator. I turned away from the window and wondered how impossible it was to understand why childbirth should be so joyful for one person, and yet such sorrow for another. The only way that I could come to terms with the inequality of it all was to trust that God knew what He was doing and that, somehow, He could bring hope and peace into every situation, even the most difficult.

I did not believe for one moment that a loving, caring God would inflict such suffering on the people He loved so dearly. It was rather the case that the world was in a sad and less than perfect state, and that the whole of creation was now prone to suffering of one sort or another. Into this chaotic and haphazard melee, I believed, God could still bring His love and healing. Jesus had come to this crazy world, and had opened the way back to God through His death on the cross. It was this bridge which He had provided which we all needed to cross in order to receive the fullness of God's gift to us.

At the end of the shift, I left the Delivery Suite feeling exhausted. I had dealt with the death of adults throughout my nursing training and, although I had never really become accustomed to it, I accepted it as the natural outcome at the end of a person's life.

The death of a baby, however, went much deeper than that. There was a terrible feeling that it was so unjust – what had that little child ever done to deserve this? And, perhaps more poignantly, it was such a waste of all that potential, of all those hopes and dreams of the parents. As I returned to my room, I knelt by my bed and wept for the little child who had lain, so alone, wrapped in green towels, never having seen the light of day.

Chapter Ten

There wasn't much time for reflection, however, as I was now entering the last few months of training and was heading towards another period of night duty on the Delivery Suite. I was looking forward to increasing my tally of normal deliveries, and perhaps the most memorable of them all came in the form of a thirteen-year-old girl.

Emma arrived on the Suite with her mother at about 10 p.m. She had been experiencing contractions for a couple of hours and was now getting uncomfortable with them. I was given the task of admitting and assessing her.

It was a strange experience. Thus far, I had only dealt with adults who were in pain, and Emma's situation opened my eyes to the fact that I really didn't know how to relate to a teenager who was going through such a major, life-changing event. How should I speak to her? Was she still a child, or was she a woman now? At thirteen, it was difficult to say.

I welcomed Emma and her mother into one of the delivery rooms. I didn't know whether she had been given any antenatal tuition, because of her unusual circumstances, or how much she understood about what was happening to her. I tried to explain everything as clearly as possible, and reassured her that we were there to help her and that she needed to trust us, and work with us. Secretly, I was dreading the time when her labour became established. I had seen (and heard) so much screaming and thrashing about by mature women as they gave birth, and I wondered just how well a young girl could cope with it all.

The hours passed, and Emma's labour gathered momentum. To my utter amazement, she did everything I asked her to do. She coped with all the monitoring equipment, the internal examinations, used the Entonox properly without screaming for any other analgesia, and was a complete star.

When the time came for the delivery itself, the first rays of sunshine were peeping over the horizon, and Emma's baby was born as the sun rose in a perfectly blue morning sky. It was only the sound of the crying of her baby that would have alerted anyone outside to the fact that this young woman was giving birth. She didn't utter one sound.

As the baby was cleaned and handed back to Emma, she welcomed him with open arms. "There you are, mum, I told you I could do it!"

Her mother had been going through agonies beside her all through the night, and the relief that it was all over flooded her face with tears. "We're keeping the baby," she explained to me. "My husband and I are going to raise him as our own, so he'll always be part of our family." I was touched by the love and compassion of that family as they coped with what must have been a very traumatic situation.

The following day, I was presented with a very different situation. A young woman from Ireland had come over to England in order to give birth to her child. She was not married, and had not been able to terminate the pregnancy because she felt that this was something she could not bear to do. So she had been staying with her sister who lived very close to the hospital.

She was admitted in early labour, and I was asked to care for her on the strict understanding that when it came to the delivery, she did not want to see or touch her baby at all. The child was to be taken straight out of the delivery room and sent to Special Care until Social Services could arrange for foster parents to care for him or her.

The situation presented me with a dilemma. As I attached the electrodes to her abdomen to check the baby's heart rate, I suddenly thought that the very sound of the monitor might make the young woman very upset. So I reduced the volume to its lowest limit, and watched the trace like a hawk, instead of listening to it, as I had become accustomed to doing.

I also found that, for the first time, it was difficult to make conversation. For most women, the painful process of giving birth is made easier by thinking about the end result – the reward for all that pain and suffering, and the culmination of months of worrying and wondering about their baby. I would usually talk to the women about names, and all their preparations, hopes and dreams. In this instance, however, the young woman did not want to talk and she turned her head determinedly away from the monitor in an attempt to block out the reality of the baby whose presence had completely challenged her life and her religious beliefs.

I really wanted to convey God's love and acceptance to this young woman. She gave me the impression that she expected everyone to condemn her because she had become pregnant. I so wanted her to know that this was not the case. If our Christian faith teaches us anything, it is that God gives us a second chance. If we make a mistake, then that is not the end of the matter – we can admit that we have done wrong, and ask for help to find a better way forward.

The labour was long and painful, made worse by the emotional pain which was permeating her mind and heart just as powerfully as the contractions took over her body. I administered as much pethidine as was possible, and helped her to use the Entonox properly. Her sister sat by her side throughout – her face filled with love and sadness. Each time it was necessary to perform an internal examination to assess progress, this was resisted and made very difficult by the mum.

When the time came for the delivery, the usual excitement was replaced by a feeling of dread. I knew that the little child who would be delivered into my hands would soon have to be whisked away, and that he or she, having heard their mother's voice from the womb, would hear it no more.

We soldiered on, and eventually, a little boy was born. He was beautiful. I clamped and cut the umbilical cord as quickly as possible, and then wrapped him in some warm towels and handed him to Wendy, who cuddled him and walked quickly with him towards the door. At that moment, the little lad snuffled and cried. I glanced at his mother, frightened that the sound would have been too much for her. Wendy did the same, and half-checked her stride. Her hand was on the door, when the young woman cried out, "No! Please don't take him away! I can't do this!"

Looking at her sister, she said, "I'm sorry, I just can't do this. Please let me keep him!"

Wendy looked at the young woman and her sister. They were hugging and sobbing together. She turned and walked slowly back to the bed. "Are you sure?" she asked.

The young woman responded by opening her arms to receive her baby son. "I just can't give him away. I'll just have to face the music at home."

Her sister was smiling now. "Don't worry about baby clothes, and things like that. I can get it all sorted out for you. You won't regret this, you surely won't."

Together they cradled the little boy in their arms, and he looked up into their eyes with a certainty that he was going to be alright, after all.

But there wasn't always a happy ending. At that time, antenatal screening was not as advanced as it is today, and sometimes the birth of a child could mean the beginning of interminable heartache for some.

At about this time, a woman in her mid-thirties was admitted to the antenatal ward with very high blood pressure. She had had a difficult pregnancy, with morning sickness so severe that she had been admitted for intravenous fluid therapy on no fewer than three occasions. She had also gone through the terrible trauma of a divorce during this pregnancy, and was facing the prospect of looking after this little child entirely on her own.

With bed rest in hospital, the pregnancy had reached 37 weeks – three short of the usual 40 weeks. The consultant in charge decided that this baby would be "safer out than in", and a caesarean section was planned. The woman was relieved, but also understandably anxious. We did all that we could to alleviate her fears, and I was given the task of escorting her to the obstetric theatre on the relevant day.

Before we entered the anaesthetic room, she grasped hold of my hand.

"What is it?" I asked.

"I'm just terrified that there is something wrong with my baby. I know it sounds stupid, but all through this pregnancy I've had this terrible feeling that there is something wrong. What am I going to do?"

I delved into my uniform pocket and brought out a clump of clean tissues (they always came in handy with all these hormones rushing through the department). Handing them to her, I tried to reassure her that she was probably just really upset because she had had an awful time throughout her pregnancy, and that she would feel much better once the baby was born. She smiled bravely, and then was wheeled into the anaesthetic room. The anaesthetist sighed loudly and looked disapprovingly at me. I held Sandra's hand until she was unconscious, and then returned to the ward.

An hour later, she returned to the ward, and the baby had been sent to Special Care. I settled Sandra back into her bed in a quiet side room, and made sure that she was as comfortable as possible. Her wound was fine, and I was hopeful that her problems would soon be coming to an end.

Half an hour later, however, I received a phone call from the Baby Unit to inform us that there were serious concerns about the baby. She seemed to be very floppy, and her appearance suggested that she might have Down's syndrome. As I replaced the receiver, I just could not believe it. How much more could one person be expected to deal with?

I kept repeating to myself the truth that many Down's syndrome children can be extremely capable and wonderful people, but it was just the fact that this lady's world had fallen apart. She had been so ill for the past nine months, her husband had left her, she was losing her home as a consequence, and had nobody to support her.

I went towards Sandra's room with a heavy heart. I popped my head around the door and saw to my relief that she was still sleeping peacefully. I placed my hand on her wrist to check that her pulse was steady, and all her other post-operative observations were fine. I left her to sleep. She was going to need all the strength she could muster to cope with this additional news.

A little while later, the consultant paediatrician arrived on the ward, asking to see Sandra. He explained that he was almost 100 per cent sure of the baby's diagnosis, and that he wanted to speak to the mum to prepare her. I explained that she was sleeping, but he insisted that it was important that he speak to her as soon as possible. I agreed to check on her progress.

When I entered the room, Sandra was lying on her back, staring up at the ceiling. For one awful moment I thought that she had died. But she looked over towards me and smiled bravely. "When can I see my baby?" she asked.

Dr Woodcoate spoke from behind me. "We will let you see her soon, Sandra, but I do need to inform you that we do have some serious concerns about your little daughter."

Sandra's face began to crumple, and I grasped her hand. She looked angrily at me. "I told you there was something wrong, didn't I?"

I smiled dumbly back, and sat down gently on the edge of her bed. I fumbled in the tissue pocket once again and helped Sandra to wipe away the tears of disbelief. She took a deep breath and looked at Dr Woodcoate once again. "What exactly is the matter with my child?"

"We are almost sure she has Down's syndrome." The doctor's voice was filled with compassion and had become husky with stifled emotion.

"Oh God! Oh no! What am I going to do?" Sandra began to weep as though the entire nine months of trauma were being released in one full torrent of emotion. I was concerned for her abdominal wound, because of the vehemence of her tears. I stroked her shoulder over and over again. "It's alright, it's alright." I repeated the words again and again in an attempt to bring some solace to a tortured soul.

Dr Woodcoate looked upset and at a loss. "I'm so very sorry. I'll come back and see you again soon, and we can discuss your daughter's condition and prognosis then." He got up to leave, but Sandra's eyes were screwed up tightly against all the barrages of an unfair world.

"Will she be alright?" Dr Woodcoate mouthed the words to me. I nodded in reply and carried on stroking Sandra's hand. Eventually, exhausted by the effort, her sobs finally began to subside. For the remainder of the evening, she was silent. I asked one of the auxiliary nurses to help her with a bed bath and to change into one of her own nightdresses.

"Sandra didn't say a word during the entire bed bath," June said. "Poor love, what is she going to do?"

"I really don't know. I wish that we could do something more to help her."

Dr Woodcoate arrived back on the ward at about eight o'clock. "How is mum doing now?"

"She is very withdrawn," I replied, and together we went into Sandra's room, where she was lying with her face towards the window.

"Your little daughter is doing very well upstairs,

Sandra, and I was wondering if you would like to see her now?"

A single tear trickled down Sandra's face, and she gently shook her head. A husky "No" was the response.

"It might help if you did see her, Sandra – she's a lovely little girl."

Sandra turned and glared at the doctor with all the dignity and strength she could muster from her vulnerable position. "I don't want to see her now, and I never will. Is that clear?"

Dr Woodcoate and I looked at each other for inspiration, but none was forthcoming. This was an entirely new situation as far as I was concerned. I'd never had to deal with something like this before, and I felt stupid and powerless to help. "I think that it would be a good idea if we gave Sandra some more time and space so that she can think about things, if that is alright?"

Dr Woodcoate nodded and quietly left the room. I turned to Sandra once again, and gently took her hand. "You have every right to be angry, Sandra. You've been through so much, and you've done so well to cope with it all. I wish that I could make things better for you, I really do."

A faint smile crossed her exhausted face. "I don't know if you, or anyone can understand how I feel. I just can't cope with a handicapped baby, not in my situation. I haven't even got a home to call my own any more, and there is nobody to help me. Nobody."

"You need time to think, Sandra. No one is here to judge you – we are just here to help you. Don't try to make any decisions about your future tonight – you are too tired. Let me settle you down to sleep, and give you something for the pain. I'm sure it will be easier to think more clearly in the morning. And meanwhile, your little girl is doing fine upstairs, and they will take good care of her."

I left the room and prepared an injection to ease Sandra's physical pain. I wished that it was as easy to deal with the emotional pain she was suffering. My mind kept wandering to the little child upstairs. I wondered if she was missing her mother and wondering where she was.

I snapped myself back to the present situation. Sandra was my first priority now. She was on her own, dealing with overwhelming emotions and fears, and she needed all the love, patience and care that we could give her. As I drew up the injection, I prayed for the wisdom to say the right thing.

As I re-entered the room, I was alarmed to find Sandra perched on the side of the bed. "I've got to get out of here. I just can't stay here another minute." In her eyes was a sadness and a palpable fear. I moved forward quickly to steady her as she wobbled precariously, drunk with fatigue and emotional exhaustion. I knew that I was going to have to be firm now in order to get her cooperation. I could feel the situation reeling out of control as rational thought seemed to be eluding her. I knew that somehow I had to provide Sandra with an anchor, a place of stability and calm if I was to prevent a worsening of an already terrible situation. For the sake of her abdominal wound it was imperative that she did not move about too much for the next couple of days.

I grasped hold of Sandra's shoulder with one hand, and with the other, pulled the red emergency cord, praying that someone would come and help me lift her gently back into bed. After what seemed an age, Belinda, one of the staff midwives arrived.

Belinda looked bemused. "Where were you trying to go, Sandra? You really need to be taking it easy for at least the next couple of days. You don't want to destroy all of the surgeon's handiwork, do you?"

Sandra was past caring now. "I couldn't give a – about any surgeon's needlework. The sooner I'm dead, the better."

Belinda looked across to me, and we both gently lifted Sandra back into bed. We checked that her wound was satisfactory, and thankfully, the sutures were intact, in spite of Sandra's bid for freedom. She must have been in terrific pain but, in spite of that, she was insisting that we let her leave the ward.

We covered her gently with the bedclothes, and I stayed with her as Belinda left to contact the senior house officer. "Stay with her, Hilary, and make sure she doesn't hurt herself."

I administered the painkilling injection and sat on the chair by the side of the bed, continuing to gently stroke Sandra's hand. Belinda's words rang a chilling bell in the recesses of my mind. Just one week previously we had received a lecture concerning postnatal psychosis – a rare, but terrifying psychological condition which made women feel that they should end their own lives after the birth of their baby.

As I looked at Sandra now, with her wild eyes unblinking, staring at the window, I felt a sense of rising panic. *Please, Lord, please bring Your peace.* I repeated the prayer over and over again in my mind and prayed that the Holy Spirit would impart the peace of God which passes human understanding. I said nothing, because there was nothing that I could say.

The minutes passed, and gradually, the injection began to take effect. Sandra's eyes became glazed and her eyelids drooped. The wild expression in her eyes gave way to a despondency, an expression of abject defeat. I felt so useless, so unable to help. I prayed silently that someone with more experience would come and rescue us both.

A couple of minutes later, a doctor I didn't recognise entered the room. "Hullo," he said quietly. "I'm Dr Barnes, duty psychiatric registrar. Would it be okay if we had a little chat, Sandra? The midwives have been telling me that you're going through a difficult patch at the moment, and we would like to help you."

Sandra continued to stare at the window.

"The doctor is here to help you, Sandra. Please listen to what he has to say."

Sandra's eyes flitted momentarily in my direction, and then she returned her gaze to the window. "Nobody can help me now," she said, with chilling finality in her voice.

Dr Barnes looked up. "I don't think that you are in any state to remain on this ward, Sandra, as it probably isn't helping that you can hear all the other babies crying. I think that we should move you down to my department, where you will receive special care, and help to work through the issues that you are faced with at the moment."

There was no response, so Dr Barnes stood up carefully, and taking Belinda outside, made arrangements for the transfer to the Psychiatric Wing of the hospital. A few moments later, Sandra was wheeled away towards the lift. I felt a terrible sense of helplessness. I wished that we had been able to help her more. I later heard that she remained in hospital for four weeks before she was helped to find a new home, and was given continuing psychiatric support in the community.

Her little girl was taken into foster care, and later adopted. I prayed that the Lord would help them both to rebuild their shattered lives.

Chapter Eleven

It was soon Christmas. As the big day dawned, I was
back pacing the floors of the postnatal ward. The few
ladies who had recently been delivered were enjoying
their rest in hospital and were thrilled to have escaped
from the supermarket trolley rage and cooking
marathons which unfortunately make Christmas such a
chore for so many.

At lunchtime, Mr Clements, one of the consul-
tants, arrived to carve the turkey in time-honoured tradition. I watched the faces of the caesarean section
ladies as knife made contact with flesh. I wondered if
they were empathising with the poor bird, but it didn't
seem to prevent any of them from eating it with great
relish.

The new year came and went with more opportunities to take charge of normal deliveries, and as the
budding green shoots of spring yielded to the summer
sun and rain, I found myself buried in revision notes
when not working on the wards. I was still living with
Cynthia, and we found that we enjoyed each other's
company and our living arrangements benefited us
both. But one morning, just before the hospital final
exams, Cynthia's health took a dramatic turn for the
worse.

She awoke looking very jaundiced, and she felt

absolutely terrible. I called her own doctor, who attended the house quickly. He referred Cynthia for an urgent scan, and an appointment was made for the next day. Richard took her to the hospital, as I was on duty at the time of the appointment. The news from the scan room was not good. A shadowy area had been located on her liver, and this strongly suggested the presence of a tumour. Cynthia was admitted to a medical ward straight away.

Richard, Deb and I were all very worried – Cynthia was such a lovely woman who was blessed with a great sense of humour and a lot of common sense. When I visited her at the end of my shift, I was horrified to see this strong-willed woman virtually melting into her bed and looking totally exhausted. She had hardly any strength for conversation, so I didn't stay for long. I went home and asked people at church to pray for her.

A few days later, she was allowed to come home, but she was under strict instructions to rest as much as possible, and to give up smoking. I did my best to look after her, but it was difficult to cope with working full time, studying for final exams, and looking after someone who was so unwell.

One evening, I went up to Cynthia's room to give her a cup of tea, and I had the strong feeling that I should pray for her and lay hands on her abdomen. I asked Cynthia if she was happy with that, and she said that she didn't care any more – she just felt too awful. I began to pray, asking the Lord to touch her in the power of His Holy Spirit, and then I placed my hands on her tummy, and stayed silent for a minute or two.

I felt my hands become hot, and a single Bible verse popped into my otherwise blank mind: "I am the

Lord, who heals you." I spoke this verse aloud to Cynthia, and then waited to see if anything else was going to happen. Nothing did, so I removed my hands, opened my eyes, and then gave Cynthia a hug. "Thanks," she said. "Can I have my cup of tea now?"

The next morning, Cynthia still looked very jaundiced, and she still was obviously very weak. I made her breakfast, vacuumed the carpets and dusted downstairs, and then left for work. Richard and Deb were due to take her for a repeat scan later on in the day.

When I returned from work, I was amazed to find Cynthia sitting up in the living room, quietly puffing on an illicit cigarette.

"How did the scan go?"

"You'll never believe it, Hilary, but they couldn't find the shadow! They kept looking for it for ages, but it just wasn't there! It's a real miracle!" Richard was overjoyed and so was I. If anyone doubted the fact that God still performs miracles today, then this was proof beyond doubt that He does.

Day by day, Cynthia's strength improved, but I was finding that the strain of caring for her when at home, together with work and studying at this crucial period of the course, was becoming too much for me. I began to feel very resentful of Richard who, now that the crisis was over, was happy to take a back seat with regards to his mother's care. In retrospect, I should have been more honest about my feelings, but instead, I let things come to a point where I announced that I would have to leave Cynthia's home.

What had been a loving and mutually beneficial friendship disintegrated into hostility and, on a summer afternoon, I handed Cynthia my month's rent and board money, packed my trunk, and left. I moved back into the Nurses' Home, which was a retrograde step, but there seemed to be no other way to cope with the situation. My grades were suffering, and I only just scraped through my hospital final exams. I needed Richard to see that he needed to be more fair about caring for his mum, and this was the only way in which I could make him do this.

A few days after the move, there was a knock at my door, and I was surprised to see Richard standing there. "You've left some of your stuff at mum's," he said.

"When would it be convenient for me to collect it?" I asked.

"You can go when you want. I hope you realise," he added, "that you have broken mum's heart by the way that you have behaved."

I felt the indignation rising in my throat. "I wouldn't have had to move out if you had been more willing to help your mum."

His face reddened with rage. "How dare you! You're nothing but a freeloader!" He was screaming in my face, and I felt fear mingling with sorrow. I could also feel that things were getting out of control. He was looking menacing, and I battled hard to steady my voice.

"Get out, please just get out!"

"Make me!" he shouted.

I raised my voice and tried to sound in control, but instead it was a high-pitched squeak. "Just get out! Get out!" I thought that, at least if I started shouting, then someone in one of the rooms along the corridor would come out, and hopefully help me. A door opened, and Richard thought twice about pursuing this further, so he turned and stormed out of the fire doors and down the stairs.

"Are you alright, Hilary?" It was Abi's voice.

"Yes, thank you. I'm okay."

But the saga was not quite over yet. I still had to return to Cynthia's to collect my few remaining belongings. I phoned to arrange a convenient time.

When I arrived at the house, I felt sick with apprehension. I was so sorry that it had all come to this. I had naively thought that, as Christians, we could work out any differences and always reach a peaceful resolution. Any hopes that this might be the case this time were soon expelled.

I knocked on the door, which was opened by Cynthia. The expression on her face was one of disgust. "Your things are in these bags," she said. Instead of handing them to me, she took them into the back garden and promptly threw all the contents over the lawn. I tried to be as dignified as possible. I moved forward to collect them, when she said, "Just one more thing", and, with that, she struck me across my face.

I recoiled in horror. What on earth had I done to deserve this? I had loved and cared for her to the extent that my own career was in severe jeopardy. Leaving the house had been my only means of making Richard assume his responsibilities towards his mother.

But this had caused problems in the family, and I was the convenient scapegoat. As a consequence, I felt that the only decent thing was to leave the church as well. The thought of so much ill-will floating around was hardly conducive to close fellowship. So I moved to a house church which met in St Albans, and hoped that, with time, the rift would heal.

I could not indulge in regret for long, however, as the state final exams were to take place in the next few days. We spent a frantic week back in college, trying to cram as much information into our jaded brain cells as possible. We were also taken through a mock *viva voce*, or oral exam, which, to me, was the most terrifying part of it all.

One by one, Miss Harrier called us into her room, where she proceeded to ask questions about any and every aspect of midwifery care for mother and baby. She had a doll and a model pelvis on her desk, and she proceeded to prod the doll in such an exaggerated fashion that I was in serious danger of losing my composure completely.

"What would you do if you found that a baby had a spot THERE?" she asked, stabbing the doll with her finger.

I rattled on about spots being a sign of infection, which should be referred to a doctor for treatment, and waffled endlessly about normal deliveries, breastfeeding, care of babies following traumatic deliveries, and what to look out for in a case of postnatal psychosis. By the end of the 20 minutes, I was perching on the edge of my chair, almost taking a nosedive into the desk which separated Miss Harrier and myself.

As I stood up to leave, my dress was sticking to me, and a small rivulet of perspiration was trickling down my back. From the mirror on the wall outside Miss Harrier's office I could see that I had turned the colour of a beetroot. I was going to have to calm down before the real exam, or I was never going to get through it successfully.

At the end of what had been a very long and difficult afternoon, we were all relieved to find that we had passed, and we decided to go to a local pub to celebrate. Some of the girls became quite merry, but we still couldn't fully relax, as in two days' time, we were going to have to do it all again, for real, in London.

We agreed to meet up to travel into London by train on the morning in question, and if ever there was a group of terrified young women en masse, then this was it. We made our way to Bonham Carter House and, in spite of my terror, I had decided that the only thing that was worse than meeting with one's fate in a strange city, was meeting it on an empty stomach. The time for the exam was twelve noon – high noon, perhaps. "I'm sorry, girls," I said, "but if I don't eat something before we go in, the examiner won't be able to hear what I'm saying above the sound of my grumbling stomach."

"Okay," they agreed, and we stopped off at a cake shop, where we ate huge Danish pastries, washed down with strong coffee. I've never been able to look at a Danish in the same way since.

We walked on to Bonham Carter House and entered the enormous hallway. We were instructed to sit in uncomfortable armchairs until our examination numbers were called. "I don't know about you," I said to Sally, "but I could do with a cylinder of Entonox now, just to steady the nerves."

Sally nodded knowingly; she looked as white as a sheet, and was biting her lower lip until its blood supply was cut off.

"Are you alright?"

"I'll be fine, when this is over."

Eventually our numbers were called. We each had to sit opposite two examiners at a desk in an enormous hall. A doll and model pelvis sat on each of the desks. I went up to my table and saw, with horror, that my examiners resembled something from a bygone age. One had her grey hair tightly twisted into a copious bun on the top of her head, and with every strand of hair pulled tightly away from her face, the impression of severity was exaggerated. The other was a very large woman, who had enormous black-rimmed spectacles which seemed to totally dominate her face. I gulped audibly as I took my seat.

Sit back in your seat, Hil, I kept telling myself, but in spite of my best efforts, I found that I was leaning further and further forwards in my eagerness to convince these women that I did really know what I was talking about. I felt that these two women had a distinct advantage over me. They had already seen and marked my written papers, and knew whether I had passed or failed them. The oral exam was to convince them that I really was worthy to be called a midwife.

Minute by minute the two formidables asked more and more questions about antenatal screening, signs of fetal distress in labour, the diabetic mother, and normal mechanisms of labour. We seemed to be finishing ahead of schedule, possibly because I was gabbling so quickly. After about fifteen minutes they stopped and looked at one another, and began to twiddle their thumbs.

Miss Harrier had told us that we could take it as a good sign if the examiners did not mention postpartum haemorrhage. "If you are asked about this, then it is likely that you have failed the exam," she had said.

The large woman peered at me over the top of her spectacles. "Well, I suppose we should ask you about how to deal with a postpartum haemorrhage." My spirits plummeted. This was it, then; I must have failed. I opened my mouth to begin to answer their question, when the bell rang, signalling the end of the session. I hesitated to leave. Was I supposed to answer the question, or not?

The dark spectacles answered my enquiring and desperate look. "That will be all. Thank you."

I felt the tears pricking my eyes. I would have to go through all this again, and I really wasn't sure that I could. I saw Sally, who had been my rival for top spot throughout the training. "How did it go?" I asked her.

"It wasn't too bad, considering."

"They asked me about postpartum haemorrhage, right at the very end. I must have failed. I can't believe it," I moaned.

Gradually, all eight of us found one another and walked out into the summer sunshine exhausted, and in my case, very disappointed. The rest of the girls were talking excitedly about their questions and checking with one another whether they had answered them correctly. I just felt completely drained, and didn't want to talk to anyone. The disappointment I felt was immense. It seemed too much for it all to come to nothing after all the hard work and studying.

I don't remember much about our journey back to Welwyn. I just followed the others onto the railway platform, and sat dumbly on the nearest seat on the train. The busy streets of London gave way to the pleasant greenness of the suburbs. I didn't try to talk to anyone because I knew that if I did, I would only embarrass them, and myself, by bursting into tears.

Back at the Nurses' Home, however, as soon as I was able to shut the door to my room, I was free to release all the feelings of disappointment and sadness which had been welling up inside since the breakdown of my relationship with Cynthia and her family. I was totally exhausted, and fell asleep with my head on a sodden pillow.

The following day I had to return to life on the postnatal ward, and to carry on as though nothing had happened. It would be another two weeks before the results were in, and I had to keep suppressing the fear of failure, and to keep my patients' present needs uppermost in my mind. I owed it to them to give them the best possible care, even if I had failed my exams.

The postnatal side of midwifery is often considered to be the "Cinderella" part of the service. It deals mainly with care of the newborn, and ensuring that neither mother nor baby succumb to any infection. Feeding is also a very large part of the care, as is the education of new mothers in the care of their new baby. But because it does not demand much of the heightened vigilance which is required when looking after ladies antenatally, nor the drama and excitement of the delivery itself, its importance can, and often is, overlooked.

After all the experiences of the previous few weeks, I was glad to be working with the mothers and their babies, and it helped me immensely to focus on these women who, due to their errant hormones, were bursting into tears even more frequently then I was. I began to love the morning sessions when I would teach all the new mothers about bathing their babies, and changing nappies, and all of the things they needed to bear in mind concerning their new charges. They were lovely, relaxed times, when the mums could ask questions, and gain confidence in handling their babies. It was very rewarding. But, at the back of my mind, I kept reminding myself that my fate would be known in just a few more days.

The night before the results were due I spent going for a long run, in an attempt to calm the jitters. I returned absolutely puce, panting, and still as nervous as a kitten. I tried to sleep, but the night was punctuated with vivid dreams of my two examiners wagging their fingers at me disapprovingly, and asking why I didn't know what to do with a postpartum haemorrhage.

When six o'clock arrived, I could bear it no longer, so I ran a huge bubble bath and spent the next hour soaking in it, pretending that this was a good way to relax. Following this, I tried to eat breakfast, but there was no milk available, and this time, I was to blame.

Two days previously, I had undertaken the task of defrosting the communal fridge, which had been so encrusted with ice that it had reduced the fridge's capacity by about a quarter. I had chiselled away at the ice, when suddenly, there was a hissing sound. I had looked with horror at where the sound was coming from, only to find that I had produced a minute hole in the wall of the fridge, and it was leaking C.F.C. gas everywhere! My immediate reaction had been to put my finger over the hole to see if this would help. After about five minutes, I came to the conclusion that it wasn't going to work, and that I was going to have to admit responsibility for the fridge's demise.

I reported the incident to the hospital authorities, and they were very gracious in acknowledging that perhaps it was time that the fridge was replaced, but that it would take a few days to arrange. Since then, all of my fellow Home mates had had to make do without fresh milk. Breakfast consequently consisted of bread and marmalade, which, considering the circumstances, was not too bad.

I tried to eat as slowly as possible, but the hands on my bedside clock seemed to be operating on a work-to-rule that morning, and no amount of my staring at it would make them move any more quickly. I tried to read my daily Bible notes, but found that I had read the first two lines at least six times before deciding that perhaps now was not the time to try reading. I closed my eyes and tried to pray, but found that the images from the previous night's dreams kept leering at me. I decided to perform some stretching exercises, but managed to hit the back of my head on the chair by the desk as I threw myself into a flurry of sit-ups.

I finally took the hint that perhaps nothing was going to work as a distraction this morning, and that I should just do the sensible thing, and wait patiently.

Nine o'clock eventually arrived, and with butterflies straight from the Amazon fluttering threateningly in my rather over-zealous gut, I made my way to the pigeonholes where our mail was deposited. With shaking hands, I reached for the mail which began with an "M" for McIntosh, but just as I did so, a rather large general nurse from the main Home placed her hand there. She turned and glared at me with an expression which spoke louder than many words. I stepped back, and had to wait a few more seconds until she had finished searching.

"Thank you," I said, when she finally returned the sheaf of letters. With another glare, she turned and walked away, leaving me alone with the letters, and a thumping heart.

Fumbling through the envelopes, I eventually found mine. It was large and white, and it stared blankly back at me, as I tried to see through it for a hint of what lay inside. I looked up at the beautiful day outside. How could bad news come on a day like this? With that hope, I took the envelope and began to walk back across the car park, fully intending not to open it until I had reached the privacy of my own room.

Halfway there, I could bear the suspense no longer,

and I tore it open. To my absolute amazement, it was a letter congratulating me on passing the state final exams.

I ran up the stairs and bumped straight into Celia, one of the other girls on my course. "Hello, Hil – have you got your results?"

"Yes, thank you," I beamed at her.

"I've got mine too. I went over to the post office when it opened at 8:30. I've passed!"

We leapt around, hugging each other warmly. It was only a few minutes later that I realised what an idiot I'd been. Whilst I had been trying to decapitate myself on the chair in my room, I could have been reading my mail, as calmly as you please.

Chapter Twelve

With the exams out of the way, the future suddenly seemed more certain and comfortable. All of my fellow students and I were offered positions as staff midwives within the Maternity Department, and we were allocated to one of the three consultant teams. This meant that we would theoretically have the opportunity to work in all areas, and to look after ladies all the way through their antenatal visits to the hospital, delivery, and then take care of them postnatally.

These were exciting times, and I felt really privileged to be working in such a unit. The staff were wonderful, and I felt respected probably for the first time in my nursing career. The only problem was that of shortage of staff. The cause of this was that Welwyn Garden City is situated in the affluent south-east of England, where house prices, even in the mid-1980s, were exorbitant. My annual salary, working full time as a midwife, was only £8,000. Consequently, nurses and midwives had great difficulty in finding affordable accommodation within reasonable travelling distance of the hospital.

It was not uncommon, therefore, to find myself on duty with only one auxiliary nurse, and one student nurse or student midwife. On some occasions, I was alone on the ward, and would have to deal with all the antenatal and postnatal ladies and their babies, do all the assessments, recordings, admissions, discharges, help with feeding, and any emergencies which arose. My role even extended to serving the meals and mopping the floors if there were any spillages. This was not quite the "extended practice" that I had envisaged!

But the thrill of my work compensated largely for the busy-ness, and I rushed around the ward, trying to give the best possible care in the shortest possible time. Perhaps things would have been a little easier had I not been transferred to the main Nurses' Home, and placed next to a girl who really enjoyed all-night parties. The combination of her antics, the thin walls, and the relentless pressure of the ward was beginning to take its toll, and the initial euphoria of having qualified as a midwife was beginning to wane.

One particular evening, I had been rushed off my feet, and had arrived back at my room at about 9:30. I was absolutely shattered, and had slumped into bed and had fallen asleep almost immediately. At about eleven o'clock, there was a sudden blast of thudding drums from next door, and the sound of a multitude of voices, shouting and cheering. I turned over and hid under the pillow, but nothing would drown out the sound.

I tried to be tolerant, and didn't want to cause a scene, but by midnight I was beginning to get really wound up. I had to be up again at 6:30 for the early shift the following day, and my patience was wearing thin. I put on my dressing gown and knocked on my neighbour's door. The volume of the music drowned out the sound of the knocking, so I tried again, this time a little harder. Again, no response. So I began to hammer on the door until someone inside eventually got the message.

My neighbour opened the door with a bottle of gin in her hand. Inside, through the smoky haze, I saw at least twelve other people, all swilling spirits straight from the bottle. "Wha's the matter?" she slurred.

"Please could you turn the music down? It's very loud, and nobody can get any sleep."

She stood looking at me with her head bobbing from side to side. I wondered exactly how many images she could see, and which one she was attempting to concentrate on. A huge smile crossed her face, and she turned to her friends. "Di' yer all hear tha'? We're making a bit of a noise, and Miss F–ing Perfect next door can't get to sleep!" There was the sound of general jeering from the group, and they all stood there, bobbing and staring at me.

"Please could you turn the music down?" I asked again.

"F– off!" she shouted, and slammed the door in my face.

I returned to my room, and wondered what on earth I should do. I knelt by the bed and talked to the One who would know how to help me. I felt rather pathetic as I poured out my troubles to the Lord. "You know the situation. Please help me to find a way through it." I felt a strange sense of peace, and I returned to bed and tried to go back to sleep.

The party eventually came to an end at about three o'clock, and for the remaining three and a half hours, I did get some rest. It was then time to get up in readiness for the early shift, which proved to be extremely busy. We had multiple admissions and discharges that morning, and all the paper work and assessments that this entails. The babies were cranky, and the mums seemed to be extra-tearful. On the antenatal side, the ladies were anxious and seemed to have more than their usual share of tears and traumas.

The phlebotomist who took the blood samples was off sick, so I also had to take all the blood samples for analysis. The parentcraft lessons had to be abandoned, because there just wasn't time to fit those into a very hectic morning. I constantly felt that I was running against the clock in order to get all the work done.

By the time the afternoon shift came on duty at one o'clock, I had almost finished everything, but it had all been done so hastily, that the Report was rather a mess. I had had so many dealings with so many people that I was confusing details from one patient to another. The girls were very understanding, and they simply read all my notes for each patient, which thankfully did make some sense, and took up where I had left off.

By the end of the shift at 3:30, I felt grey with fatigue. At the back of my mind was the nagging reminder that I was supposed to attend the Hospital Christian Fellowship party at four o'clock, and I seriously felt that I'd had enough for one day. As I sat down in my room, and removed my rather over-heated shoes, I had the insistent feeling that I really should make the effort to attend the party, in spite of how I felt.

"Seek first the kingdom of God, and all these things shall be added unto you." The verse rattled through my mind. Perhaps God had a plan for something special this afternoon, so I reluctantly washed, changed and headed for the lounge.

When I arrived there, I was surprised to see not only the five nurses and midwives who were usually present, but also a tall and very elegant young woman. She turned and said, "Hullo, my name is Janine. I'm an occupational therapist."

"Would you like a drink?" I asked. We moved over to where the drinks and cakes were laid out on one of the tables. "How long have you been at the QE II?"

"About six months. I'm living out in a house at the other side of the town. It's really lovely there."

"I bet it is," I said ruefully. "Anywhere has to be better than the Nurses' Home here."

"What's the matter with it?"

I went on to describe the previous night, and Janine's face was a picture of understanding. When I had finished, she said, "I don't suppose that you'd be interested in moving into our house, would you? It's just that one of the girls is getting married in two weeks' time, and we need a third person in order to pay the rent."

I stared at Janine in disbelief. Could this be the answer to my prayers, literally? But when I asked her how much the rent was, I was very doubtful that I would be able to afford it, having just upgraded the ancient Mini for a smart Cortina, called Rosie. "I'll have to think about this," I said. "But thank you so much for asking me."

Later in the evening, we all went to a special service at the Baptist church, where Janine proceeded to introduce me to her friends as her new housemate. Did she know something that I didn't?

When I returned to the Nurses' Home, I prayed about the situation, and began to read my daily Bible notes. As I prayed, I believe the Lord said, "I am sending you to a spacious place of blessing and refreshment, a table laden with choicest fare." If this house was the Lord's provision, then who was I to argue? The funds would come, somehow.

I contacted Janine the next day via the

Occupational Therapy Department, and we arranged that I should come and visit the house that afternoon, and meet Linda, the other housemate.

As I drove up to the house, I was struck by the beauty of the place. It was situated in a secluded cul-de-sac, and all the houses faced onto a small green where many lovely trees were in full bloom. I could not believe my eyes. It was so lovely and peaceful, and a real contrast to the concrete monotony of the hospital. I couldn't believe how therapeutic it was just to gaze at the lovely scene before me. My jagged nerves immediately felt soothed, and I felt a real sense of peace.

I found Number 10, and knocked on the door. Janine opened it whilst talking to someone on the phone. I presumed it must be her boyfriend, as she was talking so warmly and encouragingly to him. I sat down in the spacious living room, which opened out into the back garden through patio doors. I could see that the garden stretched down to fields in the distance. The greenery was lush and refreshing, and I was deep in admiration for the place when I realised that someone else had entered the room.

"Hi, you must be Hilary." Linda came forward, and we shook hands for want of a better way of introducing ourselves. Linda was shorter than Janine, and she immediately struck me as a person of integrity. She was very well spoken and obviously very intelligent, and explained that she was hoping to go into research, using her chemistry degree. At present, she was working for a local pharmaceutical company.

Janine finally finished her phone call, and then came into the living room with a tray of three coffees. "That was Adrian on the phone," she explained.

"Is he your boyfriend?" I asked, rather bluntly.

"No. He works at a conference centre near Windsor – in the neighbouring village to where my parents live. I've taken our church's young people there, and he was really helpful. He's really nice, but he's not my boyfriend."

We all talked about our backgrounds, and how we had ended up in Welwyn Garden City, and then Janine and Linda took me on a tour of the house. I was shown the smallest bedroom, which would be mine if I wanted it. It looked out onto the back garden, and it was very peaceful. I could feel a very special sense of God's presence, and after looking around the entire house and garden, I agreed that I would love to come and share the house with them. From a financial point of view, I decided, if the Lord wanted me here, then He would somehow make it possible.

We agreed that I should move in the following week, and I counted the days until I would leave the Nurses' Home. This time, I hoped that it would be for good.

The move went smoothly, and it was possible to crush all of my worldly belongings into the Cortina's spacious back seat and boot. There was just enough room for me in the driving seat, and I drove all the way there with my left arm up near my ear, resting on a tightly squeezed duvet. I prayed that I wouldn't come across any police cars, because I wasn't at all sure that it was legal to drive with absolutely no vision of the rear of the car.

Swinging the car into the beautiful cul-de-sac, I felt full of thankfulness. It was such a wonderful place, and I couldn't believe that the Lord had given me such a wonderful gift. As I bundled all my things through the front door, it immediately felt like home, and I was revelling in the luxury and freedom which that meant. Now I had space to do washing and cooking without having to walk along dark corridors, often to find my things had been stolen if they were not bolted down. I could do the ironing whenever I wished – all these things which we so often take for granted. I began to realise how exhausting living in the Nurses' Home had been, where everything seemed to be under the threat of people who really didn't care at all.

The next morning, when I woke up in my little room, I looked out of the window over the fields. There was a weeping willow tree at the foot of the garden, and past that, there was a narrow fence which opened out onto verdant meadows. What was it the Lord had said? "I am leading you to a spacious place ... " His word was coming true.

It made me realise just how important obedience is in our relationship with God. If I hadn't bothered to attend the H.C.F. tea on the afternoon following that fraught night, then I might never have known about this wonderful place, and these lovely people. I began to see that He was able to work through the unpleasant and difficult events of our lives. Very often, it is those events which throw us on His mercy, and open our eyes to His purpose and plans for us.

As the days passed, I began to get used to my housemates' particular habits. Janine, for example, took the quickest baths I have ever known, whereas Linda liked to soak for a couple of hours with a good book. We learned to take turns in the kitchen for cooking, and sometimes ate together, depending upon shift patterns. It was a system which worked well, and I loved the spaciousness and freedom which the house gave to us all.

Work continued to be very busy and challenging,

and I was delighted to be trained up to work in the obstetric theatre as a scrub nurse there. This meant that I could now assist the doctors during emergency or elective caesarean sections, and it added a new dimension to an already very varied job description.

The day after I had finished my theatre training, an emergency arose in one of the delivery rooms. I was called away from the postnatal ward by Sister Jenkins, to scrub up and prepare theatre "as soon as you humanly can!" I rushed down the long corridor, and whirled into the changing rooms on the Delivery Suite. Tearing off my uniform, I hopped around on one leg in my haste to get into the theatre "blues" – a loose cotton top and trouser set, worn under the sterile green gowns in the operating theatre. I found a pair of theatre clogs, and grabbing a paper hat, clip-clopped rapidly towards the theatre.

I tied a face mask on and ripped open the theatre trays which lay ready in preparation for any obstetric emergency. I scrubbed my arms and forearms with a liquid iodine preparation, and could hear the patient's trolley being wheeled into the anaesthetic room next door. I knew that I only had a couple of minutes in which to get everything ready.

I rushed back to the trolley, unwrapped the inner layer, and took out the theatre gown. Slipping it on, I shrugged it over each shoulder, taking care not to touch the outer aspect of the gown, because this could potentially pass microbes on to the mother or baby during the procedure. At that moment, Sandie, one of the other midwives, came in, and tied up the gown. She opened my gloves, and my hands were shaking as I tried to put them on.

I could hear the anaesthetist calling for "cricoid

pressure" from his assistant, and I knew that any second, my patient would be wheeled through the double doors, and the surgeons would be expecting all their instruments to be at hand. They were busily scrubbing up and their voices were raised in agitation. "We're going to have to be quick this time. The fetal trace looks very dodgy."

I set up some of the swabs on forceps and counted all the remaining swabs. It was imperative that we had an accurate count at the beginning of the procedure to ensure that none were left inside the patient. I placed the retractor and all the scalpels, scissors, diathermy and suturing material in order on the trolley, and the patient was whisked in.

The obstetric registrar who was performing the operation stood opposite.

"You're new to this, aren't you?"

"Yes I am, Dr Akbar."

"Well, we need to get this baby out quickly, so you'd better be on your toes."

I tried not to let his attitude affect my performance in any way, and simply set about handing him the instruments as quickly as possible, anticipating his every move. As the uterus was cut, the fluid surrounding the baby gushed over the trolley and the floor. Instead of being clear, it was a greenish colour, a sure sign of fetal distress.

Within seconds, Dr Akbar was holding the baby's head, and attempting to release it from the uterus. It immediately became apparent that the umbilical cord had become wrapped tightly around the baby's neck. A few agonising seconds passed as he attempted to release the cord, but it was very tight, and the baby very slippery.

"Hand me some clamps!" he almost shouted.

I handed him two clamps, and had some cord scissors at the ready. It took several seconds to apply the clamps as the cord was stretched around the baby's neck, and there was very little gap between each of the three loops. I stood silently praying for the little child whose expressionless face was turning a very dusky shade of blue. *Please let him be alright. Please, Lord, let this little child be alright.*

After what seemed an age, but was only a few seconds, the cord was cut, and Dr Akbar was releasing the upper, and then the lower shoulders, and the rest of the baby's body escaped from the uterus with slippery ease. He handed the baby to the paediatrician, who was looking anxious. The baby was rushed to a resuscitation trolley, and the paediatrician and Special Care sister set to work to help the little child to breathe.

Meanwhile, Dr Akbar was delivering the placenta, and was soon ready to begin suturing. I was anticipating all his moves, and the entire procedure was completed in just under fifteen minutes. I counted all the swabs as the wound was closed, and did the same with the instruments.

The baby was beginning to breathe on his own, and his colour was definitely improving. I kept glancing to where he lay, and it was an incredible relief when he began to cry. There was a collective sigh of relief in the theatre, and the strained, anxious faces of the health professionals gave way to a collective grin.

The baby was wrapped in warm blankets, placed in an incubator, and taken up to Special Care. I thanked God for looking after us all, and for the ways in which we were now able to preserve life when, in previous generations, this situation would have resulted in not only the death of a baby, but also quite possibly the death of the mother.

Dr Akbar looked across the table at me. "Not bad for a first time, eh?"

"Thank you," I said. "I thought you were trying to break the world record for performing a caesarean section."

"Well, if we keep going like this, then perhaps we shall stand a chance of it!" He laughed as he removed his theatre gown, and then sauntered off to write up the medical notes. The theatre was suddenly very empty, and I realised that, having done all the dramatic stuff, I was now left with the very laborious process of washing everything up.

Chapter Thirteen

Life couldn't have been busier. When not at work, I was either at home or out playing badminton at the local health centre. I had been invited to join the local club which took part in county club games. When not playing there, I played at Shenley Hospital with a group which largely consisted of Indonesian men who were extremely good players.

I love the game because it is challenging at every level, and whether you are an absolute beginner or much more experienced, it is so much fun. It was a great way to vent frustrations after a pressurised day on duty. Whacking the shuttlecock a few dozen times did wonders for one's state of mind.

I never did aspire to the levels of my Indonesian opponents, however. They would laugh at my attempts to reach their impossible lobs and drop shots, and I would leave the games exhausted and completely outclassed.

Church life was going well, too. The house church which I had joined was vibrant and had a real family atmosphere. The times of worship were very precious, and I felt very close to the Lord there. One of the house groups from the church met a few metres away from the hospital, and I used to go to the weekly meetings with a great sense of anticipation. You never really knew what would happen next.

One evening, as everyone arrived, we all sat down as usual, and sang a few worship songs together. Then, one by one, we went around the group describing one thing which we had seen as an answer to prayer during the past week, and one other thing for which we would like the others to pray.

A slightly older couple, Jill and Bob, seemed very quiet and upset, and when it came to their turn to speak, they were both very near to tears. Their neighbours were giving them a terrible time, constantly playing very loud music into the small hours, and verbally abusing them whenever they met in the street.

Sam, the leader of the group, suggested that we should all gather around Jill and Bob, and begin to pray for God's protection and peace for them. We all started to pray, and placed a hand on their shoulders. I could feel the presence of the Lord like an insistent gentle breeze on my right side, which was comforting and empowering at the same time.

Being a rather quiet member of the group, I struggled with the increasingly urgent feeling that I should open my mouth and begin to pray aloud. For a minute or two, I battled with the feeling, hoping that somebody far more experienced in this sort of thing would speak up instead.

Those two minutes passed, and I felt that if I didn't say something, then I would probably burst. There was nothing for it, I was going to have to pray aloud, but what on earth was I going to say? A tiny, squeaky voice escaped from my tight throat: "Lord, please help Jill and Bob with their neighbours." My heart was thumping wildly, but I couldn't understand why. And then it was as though the flood gates were opened, and I began to pray with insight into their situation, and that of their neighbours, with knowledge that I could not have humanly acquired.

From head to foot, I was shaking in a way that I had not experienced before. It felt as though my entire being was connected to some terrific source of energy. I felt rather overwhelmed and opened my eyes. Sam was standing opposite me with his wife, Liz. "Keep going, Hilary," he said. "The Lord is anointing you to pray with authority and power in His Name. Keep going."

I gulped audibly, and felt completely out of my depth, but I closed my eyes and continued to pray, declaring Christ's victory over sin and evil on the cross, releasing those bound in difficult circumstances, and proclaiming Jesus' resurrection power.

When the vivid images which had passed in front of my closed eyes eventually ceased, I stopped praying. A wonderful sense of peace seemed to fill the room, and my thumping heart eventually quietened down.

We stood in silence for a couple of minutes, and I began to feel rather embarrassed. Had I gone on too long? Had I said the right things? I was beginning to feel that perhaps I had been too bold. What right did I have to pray in such a way? But it hadn't been just me. The Lord had given me the words and the understanding, albeit for just a few glorious minutes, and I believed that He had authority over all evil as a result of His crucifixion and resurrection. He tells us in the Bible that we are to use this power to carry on the work which He began when He walked the earth 2,000 years ago.

The silence was broken by Liz's ever practical suggestion. "Come on, girls. Let's go and put the kettle on."

We filed into the kitchen, leaving the menfolk to

contemplate some important issue or other. Liz filled the kettle, and as she did so, I once again felt an incredible surge of God's power passing through my being. "Liz!" I half whispered. "It's happening again!"

She looked at me, a little puzzled, but when she saw my trembling hands, she seemed to understand. "That means that the Lord still has something to say to us. Start praying, everyone."

We all closed our eyes, and once again, the images of people's situations and Jesus' love and healing power appeared before my closed eyes. I began to pray for each person in the room and, to my amazement, some slumped to the floor under the anointing power of the Holy Spirit. I prayed for each one of them, asking the Lord to complete the work which He was so obviously doing in each person's life.

Sometimes, there was a word or a sentence which I passed on to a person, and each time it seemed to be of some significance. I could not have possibly known about the relevance of these words by myself, and it was as though the Lord was speaking to each and every person there in a code which was of relevance to them alone.

After an hour and a half, probably the longest time ever taken to make a pot of tea, one of the men came into the kitchen and found us all huddled on the floor, in fits of laughter. The incredible life, power, healing, exuberant joy and love of Jesus had completely bowled us all over, and we were laughing out of sheer joy and thanksgiving to a wonderful God.

Jack returned to the other room and told the men that that if they wanted a drink then they had better be willing to make it for themselves. They sidled into the kitchen, carefully stepping over the prostrate forms of some of the ladies who were still resting in the Spirit, and put the kettle on, making drinks for us all. After a while, we calmed down and finished the evening with a cup of tea and a slice of cake.

As I walked home, I could still feel the buzz of energy coursing through every fibre of my being. It was as though the Lord was reassuring me that He was still there, and that all would be well. But that night I found it very difficult to sleep. I couldn't forget the incredible experience of seeing God in action. To have felt that wonderful, holy power was a tremendous privilege, and I spent most of the night kneeling by my bed, in awe of His goodness and mercy.

I wondered if life would ever be the same again. But the following day, I was back on the wards, running up and down, answering the various buzzers, and wishing that I had more than one pair of hands. As so often happens after a time of spiritual blessing, there followed an attack from the opposition. This time, it came in the form of one of the senior midwives.

Mrs Singleton was a short, middle-aged woman who, on the surface, seemed pleasant enough. When crossed, however, her true character was readily exposed. On this particular day, I was the unfortunate individual to reveal her nastier side.

I had arrived on the ward ten minutes before my shift was due to begin, only to be greeted with the information that there was absolutely nobody to work with me, not even an auxiliary or student nurse. There were two new post-operative cases, still on intravenous therapy and requiring strong analgesia which had to be checked by two members of staff. There were also many newly delivered mothers who were struggling to feed their babies. On the antenatal side, there were several ladies who had been admitted for bed rest because of pre-eclampsia of varying degrees, and there were several more ladies who were in early labour.

After Report, I decided that the ward could not be adequately managed by only one person – it would take at least two midwives to cope with this amount of work, and the implications, should anything go wrong, did not bear thinking about. If there was an emergency, for example, then I didn't even have a person who could get to the phone to summon help.

Consequently I decided that I should inform the senior midwives of the situation. I went to their office in person because I felt it would be better to discuss the situation in private, and out of earshot of the patients. I knocked on the door and was greeted by the customary "Come!" I entered the room and shut the door.

"What is it?" Mrs Singleton's voice was sharp with impatience. I could see that she had already had enough for one day, but this didn't change the situation on the ward, and I took a deep breath and waded in.

"I really feel that the staffing situation on the ward is not adequate for this afternoon's shift. Please could you call in some help from the agency?"

Sonia Singleton looked up from her desk with an expression of sheer disbelief on her face. "Do you think we're made of money?" she asked, the anger slicing through her words with great precision.

"No. But I do believe that our patients need a high-quality service." My bluntness came as a shock to both of us.

"Well," Mrs Singleton replied, "the way I see it is this. You are a newly qualified midwife, full of ideals and good ideas. But," she continued, "I think that really it's time you came down to earth and realised that the real world isn't all that we want it to be. You can't just go demanding help whenever you feel like it. If you can't cope with the situation, then you're no use to us here." Her neck and face were reddened with fury, and she glowered at me from her desk.

"But this situation is far from ideal. Suppose there was an emergency … ?"

"Like I say, if you can't cope, then perhaps you are in the wrong job. Now get back to your ward. I will not put up with any more of this."

I fumbled my way out of the office, half apologetically, half lividly. What right had this woman to deny the patients adequate staffing levels? I spoke to Sister Ruby on my return to the ward. "What am I going to do? Supposing something goes wrong? It will be seen as my responsibility, and I will be blamed for it. I just can't win in this situation."

"I'll stay on duty with you until half past five; that's as late as I can manage, but at least it will give you some time to get the new post-op ladies off their I.V.s, and I'll help you to complete the afternoon postnatal checks."

I could have hugged her. We both knew that this was going to be a labour of love for her as there was no way that she was going to be paid overtime for doing two extra hours' work. I accepted her offer with gratitude, and we set about completing all the checks in record time.

We were making good progress until I came across a young woman who had delivered her baby the previous afternoon. She was distraught.

"Maria, what's the matter?" I asked, quite unnecessarily, because the answer was plain to see. Her little boy was obviously ravenous, and she had been attempting to feed him almost without a break for the whole day. Consequently, she was getting very sore, and the baby only stopped sucking in order to yell frantically before latching on and trying to feed again.

It was all getting rather desperate: the baby, whose only concern was to fill his tummy, and the mother, who was desperately trying to meet her little boy's needs. It is an unfortunate fact of nature that a mother's milk does not fully flow until two or three days after the delivery, and these days are sometimes fraught with feelings of inadequacy and desperation, especially when the baby is large, and the mother has had a long and difficult labour.

Maria looked exhausted. "Let me take him for a moment," I said. I picked up the little child and wrapped him in a blanket, and jiggled him about whilst walking up and down the room. I talked to him quietly, and gradually, he began to calm down. When I returned to Maria's bed, I found that she had fallen asleep, completely exhausted by the entire combination of events.

I placed the little bundle in his perspex cot and wheeled him out into a small alcove next to the midwives' station, explaining to the lady in the next bed exactly where the baby was, so that when Maria awoke, she would not be worried.

The little lad thought about starting another bout of crying, and then exhaustion seemed to get the better of him as well, and he went to sleep in his new, rather cosy location. I rushed up and down the ward, completing the postnatal checks, and keeping an ear open for any footsteps along the ward to ensure that nobody walked away with the baby.

Sister Ruby and I bed-bathed both of the post-caesarian section ladies, and removed their catheters and drips as they were now tolerating oral fluids well. They were looking much more comfortable after we had administered intra-muscular analgesia, and then, all too quickly, the time had come for Sister to leave.

"Best of luck, Hilary!" she called as she rushed out of the ward.

"I think I'll need more than luck," I muttered in response. I swallowed hard to quell the rising feeling of panic which had an uncanny knack of starting somewhere in the gut region and then progressing with frightening speed and accuracy to the legs and arms. I hated this feeling of impending doom. I knew that I needed someone else on the ward to help, but there was absolutely nobody available and, try as we might, we couldn't simply pluck an extra midwife from thin air.

The buzzers started going, and I rushed around like the proverbial chicken trying to help as many people as possible. Whilst flying past the midwives' station, the phone began to ring. I rushed to the bay where the buzzer was ringing to ensure that it wasn't an urgent request, and finding that it was a mum wondering if she should change her baby's nappy, I told her to go ahead, and then returned to the phone. The voice on the other end took me completely off guard.

"Hello," it said. "This is the path lab. I'm calling with some urgent b-b-b-b-b-blood test results."

I thought that someone was pulling my leg. I tried to sound professional, and simply said, "Oh yes, and which patient are these results for?"

"They're for B-B-B-B-B-Beverley Moorhouse."

"Ah, I see, I'll just get a pen and write them down." Even as I did so, I could feel the corners of my mouth beginning to twitch. "I've got the pen; please go ahead."

"White b-b-b-b-b-blood cells ... " By now I was doubled up, and had to place my hand over the mouthpiece to stifle the hysterical giggles which were erupting of their own accord. Each time he gave me the number of the relevant blood cells, I wrote them down, took a deep breath and said, "I've got that; what's next, please?"

By the end of the call, my voice was about two octaves higher than normal, and I felt terribly guilty because the poor man must have known that I was beside myself with laughter because of his unfortunate speech impediment. It seemed a rotten twist of fate that a person who had such difficulty in producing words which began with the letter "B" should find himself constantly talking about blood.

Once the call had finished, I felt weak with laughter, so I collapsed on the chair at the midwives' station, and tried to gather some form of composure. No sooner had I sat down, than the phone began to ring again. It was the senior house officer asking for the blood results which I had just received.

My voice must have sounded rather odd because Dr Silcoates asked, "Are you alright, Hilary? It's just you sound a little strange."

"If you were having the type of evening I'm having, then you might sound a little strange, too," I replied. I took another deep breath and relayed the relevant information to her.

"That's okay then; I think we don't need to call the registrar. We'll complete some more tests in the morning. Have a good evening!" And with that, she hung up.

I sighed to myself, and three buzzers went off simultaneously, which resulted in the awakening of the baby in the alcove who had suddenly remembered that his tummy was empty, and where was his mother, anyway? I wheeled him back to her bedside. "I'm sorry that you didn't get much sleep, but I hope that you're feeling a little better."

She turned over, bleary-eyed. "Thanks, anyway," she said and she prepared herself for another onslaught from the ferocious gums of her little son.

"Would you like to try him with a bottle, just until your milk comes in?" I asked.

"I'm determined to give him only breast milk," she replied, grimacing as bony gum met raw flesh.

"Are you sure?" I asked.

"Oh, go on then. It won't do him any harm, will it?"

"Let's put it this way," I said. "If he keeps going like this, by the time your milk arrives, you're going to be bleeding so much that he won't be able to feed. This way, at least you get a chance to recover, and he has a chance to fill his tummy. Sounds like a good idea to me."

I warmed a bottle of milk, and handed it to Maria. The baby didn't need any persuasion – he was ravenous, and drank the complete bottle in less than five minutes. He gave an enormous burp, filled his nappy, and went swiftly back to sleep. I left Maria tucking him into his little cot, and then flopping back into bed herself to catch up on all the sleep she had lost.

Tomorrow would be another day, and her milk would stand much more of a chance of coming in if she had some proper rest. I struggled with the purists' view that a baby should never, ever, under any circumstances be given formula milk. What was a mother in Maria's circumstances supposed to do?

Another buzzer sounded from further up the cor-

133

ridor where the two post-operative ladies were waiting patiently.

"We're really sorry," they said, "but we really need to have a wee."

"I'll be with you in just one moment. I've just got to summon help from the other ward so that we can lift you onto a bedpan."

I flew to the phone, and found an auxiliary nurse who was willing to help. We lifted the two women as carefully as possible, freshened them up, and settled them back down to sleep.

I had just finished in the sluice, when the phone rang again, and this time it was the staff in the Special Care Baby Unit. Both of the section babies were doing well, and the staff wanted to discharge the babies down to their mothers. I explained that I was alone on the ward, and if the mothers wanted to care for their babies, they would need someone to help them, so they sent down one of the nursery nurses with the babies, and she cared for them on the ward for the remainder of the shift.

Meanwhile, on the antenatal side, one of the mothers buzzed me to say that she was getting some pain. She was due to give birth within the next week, but had been admitted early as a precaution, because her previous delivery had taken all of seven minutes, from start to finish. When I realised who she was, I hastily escorted her to her bed, and grabbed an examination trolley on the way. Her husband was visiting at the time. "Please be quick!" he said, rather unnecessarily I thought. "She was very fast last time!"

"I know – I've read the notes."

The examination took all of ten seconds, and revealed that after only three contractions, Tracey's cervix was already seven centimetres dilated. There was no time to lose. I grabbed a wheelchair from the day room, encouraged Tracey to sit in it as quickly as was decently possible, scribbled the quickest examination findings in the notes, contacted the Delivery Suite, and told the nursery nurse to press the emergency ward buzzer if anything went wrong in the time that I was away from the ward.

I swung the wheelchair through the double doors and turned left down the Delivery Suite corridor, instructing the husband to run ahead and open all the doors which might impede our progress.

"Oh no, here comes another one!" I hoped that Tracey was referring to another contraction, rather than the baby itself, and I almost mowed down Sister Gregory in my haste to find an empty delivery room. We burst into room number three, and I half carried Tracey onto the delivery bed.

"Ooooh!" she said, as women tend to when they're about to give birth. It's a particular kind of moan, and as soon as you hear it, you know that you'd better get your gloves on – the quicker the better.

Sister Gregory took the hint and, even as I turned to leave the room, I could hear her saying, "Now, Tracey, I don't want you to push; you must pant as the baby's head is coming out."

As I marched up the corridor with my empty chariot, I heard the baby giving its first cry. It amazed me that some people could experience labour in its entirety in the time it took to boil a kettle, whilst others staggered on, sometimes for days at a time, before finally receiving their bundle of joy.

Back on the ward, the buzzers were going 19 to the dozen. One of the antenatal ladies was most apologetic.

"I'm really sorry," she said, "but I've been on this monitor for an hour and a half, and I really need the bathroom."

I apologised, explaining that the trace should only have taken half an hour in the first place, and that I'd had to deal with a few urgent events. As I looked at the trace from the monitor, however, I realised that this lady was also in labour, having contractions every two to three minutes. "I really need to examine you first, before you nip to the loo."

"It's okay, I just feel that my bowels are very full, and I need to have a really good clear-out."

I'd heard this before, when a mother of twins was on the Delivery Suite, and I was still a student. Sister Choi had reprimanded me for giving the lady a bedpan, when in actual fact, her babies were about to be born. I had lost the privilege of delivering the twins as a result.

Another quick examination revealed that Sandra was about five centimetres dilated, and the baby's head was very low in the birth canal. There must have been something in the air that night, as it seemed that all the ladies were labouring remarkably quickly. I called Delivery Suite again, and Sister Gregory answered the phone. "What are you doing to these women, Hilary?"

"Nothing that I'm aware of, Sister; it's just one of those things."

"I believe you." I could hear the smile in her voice. "Thousands wouldn't."

Another trip to the Delivery Suite with hubby, suitcase and washbag in tow, and then another dash back to the ward. When I arrived there, I found the first of the night staff sitting at the station. "It can't be that time already, can it?" I gasped.

"It sure is, honey," Thelma replied. She was a large,

motherly Jamaican woman, whose very voice could calm the most agitated mother or baby. She always seemed so peaceful, and I could never imagine her being anything other than that. I wished that it was possible to patent her secret.

I ran through the Report, filling in the notes as I went.

"It's okay, honey, we'll catch up with anything that hasn't been done. You get away home to your bed, and we'll see you in the morning."

"Thanks, Thelma, you're an angel."

"Can you see my halo, girl? 'Cos I sure can't!"

I smiled and blew her a kiss, and headed out of the ward. My feet were stinging in protest, and my left shoe had started to creak. What a day! And tomorrow, well, it could be more of the same.

Chapter Fourteen

Back at the house, Janine was coming up with plans for a grand social evening. She was an enthusiastic member of the local Gilbert and Sullivan Society, and had connections with numerous musicians. As a result, she decided that it would be rather grand, and fun, to host a May ball, with a string quartet playing in the dining room, and disco music playing in the living room. The dress would be formal, with the men wearing black tie, and the ladies in long dresses.

At first I felt rather daunted by the prospect. Janine knew a lot of people, and the number of guests which we eventually invited totalled nearly 70. We warned the neighbours that we would be hosting the party, and that we would try to keep the noise down to a dull roar. They were surprisingly acquiescent about the whole thing, and I think that they went out for the evening, which solved any problems.

Janine, Linda and I spent the entire day preparing party food, and by the time the first guests arrived at seven o'clock, the table was fully laden. A huge punch-bowl was at its centre, filled to the brim with fresh fruit and a mixture of exotic fruit juices. It wasn't long before the first guests arrived.

Amongst them was Janine's friend, Adrian, and his friend, Steve, who lived near to the conference centre at

Dorney, near Windsor. They walked into the house looking extremely smart. I did notice, however, that the rules concerning black tie had been altered slightly, and that Adrian was wearing a pale blue suit, with pink shirt, tie and socks – an interesting combination.

But that was nothing compared to the point when the dancing began. To this day, I cannot believe how anyone could dance so animatedly within such a confined space – there were arms and legs everywhere! At one point, Adrian managed to do the splits in mid-air, and looked every inch a serious contender for the Russian ballet.

When the quieter music came on, he walked over to the window where I was standing. "Would you like to dance?" he asked.

"I must warn you that I've got a cold at the moment," I replied.

"Oh, well, I'll take my chances."

And with that, we began to dance together. It felt strange but lovely to be dancing closely with someone again. I hadn't really entertained the thought of having a boyfriend since my breakup with Alan, who had been my boyfriend in Edinburgh, and I kept telling myself not to get too carried away – this was, after all, only a bit of fun.

The dance came to an end, and he bowed low and I curtsied, and then we went to get a glass of punch from the dining room. The string quartet were playing on heroically, battling against the louder music which emanated from the other room. It was a lovely light evening, so Adrian and I went out into the back garden, and talked about life in general. Every time I looked at him, I could sense that here was a man who was full of life and fun, and yet who had experienced pain as well.

He explained that he ran a conference centre which catered for groups of underprivileged children who came to spend a week at a time away from the difficulties of inner-city life in London and Oxford. The centre was supported by the local church, and Adrian explained that he had to use all of his gifts, both practical and spiritual, to keep the centre going. He said that although the work was exhausting, it was also very rewarding.

I listened as he talked, and I thought that it was wonderful that someone should do this sort of work. It seemed unlike any other occupation that I had come across, and I felt that it must take someone with great commitment and patience to deal with groups of eight- to eleven-year-olds as they coped with being away from home for the first time.

"Hil, can you come and make some more punch?" Janine's voice broke through our conversation.

"Sure ... I'll just have to go and get that sorted out," I said to Adrian. "It's been lovely talking with you." I stood up and went indoors, and Adrian went back to his dancing in the living room.

The party eventually came to an end at about 2:30 a.m., and as the last guest left, Janine, Linda and I heaved a huge sigh of relief. We'd had a great time, but there was a full day's work ahead of us in clearing up the remnants of our wonderful evening. We decided that we would go to bed for a few hours before embarking upon the marathon clean-up, but before I could settle down to sleep, I had this nagging feeling that the Lord wanted to tell me something. I'd felt this insistent presence before, and I knew that when this happened, it was useless to ignore it.

I groaned as I knelt down beside the bed. *Okay, Lord, what is it that You want to tell me?*

As clear as day the words came into my mind: *You know Adrian?*

Yes. Did You see the way he was dancing?

Yes. Well, he is the man I want you to marry.

I started to laugh. I must be hearing things. *I'm sorry, Lord, I'm really too tired to talk any more. Can we speak again in the morning?*

With that, I fell into bed and wasn't conscious of anything else until six hours later. When I awoke, however, I felt a strange question mark in my heart. Had God really been speaking to me about Adrian, or was it my imagination? I decided to pray about it all some more. The strange thing was, that the more I prayed about Adrian, the more the Lord revealed to me about him. It was almost as if my heart was being prepared for this relationship even before we spent any further time together.

The days passed, and I continued to feel this insistent sense of anticipation in my heart. I kept praying, and asking the Lord what I was supposed to do next. I couldn't just call him and say, "By the way, Adrian, remember me from the May ball? Good, well the Lord has told me that we are supposed to get married!" Somehow, I didn't really think that this was the right approach!

I felt at a loss as to what to do next. I had always been brought up to believe that the man should make the first move in a relationship, but if the man in question was 45 miles away, there needed to be some way of instigating proceedings. So, in a moment of boldness, I decided to write Adrian a letter. In it, I told him that I admired his work very much, and that I thought that he was a lovely person. I sealed the letter and, with thumping heart, posted it quickly, before the adrenalin had time to fade.

I had sent the letter first class, and the next morning, when I knew that the letter should have arrived, I felt a combination of guilt, horror, disbelief and excitement. Supposing I had got it all wrong? Perhaps I had been a total idiot, after all.

This negative train of thought escalated over the following few days, when I didn't receive any response at all. Then, worst of all, Adrian rang the house and asked to speak to Janine, and not to me. He was asking her for advice about going to Geneva for a few days. Janine gave him all the advice he needed, and then hung up.

I felt desperately disappointed. I'd obviously made a big mistake, and I secretly thanked God that at least I hadn't told anyone about the letter. I threw myself into work once again, and tried to forget about the man I hardly knew, but who was mysteriously taking root in my heart.

The weeks passed, and then in the middle of August, when I thought that it had all come to nothing, Adrian rang again.

"Hi!" Janine shouted from the hall. "It's for you!"

"Who is it?"

"It's Adrian." She passed the receiver to me with a grin on her face. I tried to sound casual and calm, but it's not easy when your heart is making a bid to leap out of your chest.

"Would you like to come over to the centre at the weekend so that you can see the work, first-hand?"

I couldn't believe it, but agreed to go, and from that moment on, the weekend could not come quickly enough. I hardly slept on the Friday night. I was panicking about getting lost on the journey, and those who know me well know that this was not without reason. If I do get lost, I am seldom able to find the right way once again, so I lay in bed, memorising the route, and fending off the visions of ending up in Wales at the end of the M4.

The time came to leave and, armed with a large, idiot-proof map book, I set off on my new adventure. Miraculously, I didn't get lost, and arrived at the centre on time.

As I swung the Cortina through the gates and parked on the gravel drive, I was taken aback by the beauty of the place. The centre itself was a large and quite imposing white building with black, Tudor-like beams across its façade. It stood in spacious grounds and was surrounded by numerous old trees which sheltered it from the main road.

As I parked, Adrian appeared from the back of the building where his flat was situated. We went inside the house, and he showed me each of the many rooms. Upstairs, the old bedrooms had been transformed into a very interesting array of dormitories of different sizes, which could accommodate up to 25 people. Downstairs, the dining room was situated in the part of the house which was nearly 400 years old, and it had a very low, beamed ceiling. The house was full of character, like the man who was showing me around.

After a cup of coffee in Adrian's bachelor flat, we went into Slough for some shopping. As we were walking, Adrian took hold of my hand, and it felt as though this was how it was meant to be, a complete feeling of rightness and peace. In my heart I was thanking God, while on the outside, I was trying to play it cool, but probably failed miserably!

We then drove to the riverside, and walked along the tow path, past Boveney Lock, smiling and waving at all the people in their smart boats, as they basked in the summer sunshine, gently chugging up and down the Thames. It was so beautiful, and several swans flew majestically by, fanning their great wings, and shooting out their marvellous feet as they came to land on the surface of the water.

Adrian and I talked about life in general, about faith, our work, our families and friends. The time seemed to pass so quickly, and it wasn't long before we returned to the flat to get changed in readiness for our trip to Esher. Linda's family lived there, and we had been invited to her sister's birthday party.

When we arrived, the party was beginning to get under way. Linda took me to one side. "How's it going with Adrian?" she whispered.

"Oh, fine, I think, thank you."

"My sister has just asked when you're getting married!" She shrieked with laughter, and I just smiled and said nothing. Perhaps my feelings for Adrian were more than just a figment of my imagination, after all.

As the party came to an end, we drove back to Dorney through darkened streets and brightly lit motorways. His Marina was a powerful car with a "pudding basin" gear lever – so named because when you tried to change gear, it was a bit like stirring a mixture in a basin – you took potluck as to which gear you eventually found.

It was almost midnight by the time we arrived back, and Adrian set up an air bed on the floor of his living room for me to sleep on. "Will that be okay?" he asked.

"That will be fine, thanks."

We both hesitated as he was about to say good-night, and then he turned to me again. "Oh, blow it!" he exclaimed, so romantically. "May I kiss you?"

That first kiss was like the melting of two souls into one, an incredible sense of peace and joy, as though my soul had found its resting place, its support and its friend. We eventually came up for air, and decided that we really should get some sleep, because the church service the following morning was due to begin at 9:30, and it was one o'clock by now.

We said goodnight, Adrian went off to his bed, and I lay down on the inflatable mattress on the floor. My mind was racing. I was so excited, so thrilled to be here – it was all so lovely, but at the same time, part of me was advising caution, and not to rush in where angels fear to tread.

As I lay listening to the sane voice, I became aware of other voices. They were coming from a doorway at the end of the living room, which led through to one of the smaller dormitories. In that room, three young men from Eton College, who were helping with the children who were on holiday at the time, were talking together, deep into the night.

"Do you think that Adrian and his girlfriend will be doing it tonight?" one voice asked.

"I don't know," said another, then, following a moment's reflection, "quite possibly!" This was followed by some general "whooooas" and "hey heys", and I could feel myself blushing to the point of almost glowing in the dark. Little did they know.

Eventually their conversation came to an end, and I fell into a disturbed sleep – disturbed mainly because the inflatable mattress was very narrow, and every time I turned over, I rolled onto the floor. By the morning, I felt rather the worse for wear, but we had breakfast and headed off down the lane to the church.

I hadn't really thought much about the church itself. I was used to worshipping in a school hall, and the services sometimes lasted for hours, going wherever the Spirit led. As we turned the corner in the lane, and crossed the road, the ancient little church with its square tower suddenly came into view. "It dates back to the twelfth century," Adrian explained.

We turned right, into the tiny graveyard, and then entered the church under a very low porch at the side of the building. It was like stepping back in time. The wooden pews and flagstones were worn with centuries of use by faithful pilgrims. The stained glass windows were small, giving the church a cloistered atmosphere. The air was heavy with the passage of time, and smelled musty, in spite of the vases of fresh flowers which adorned some of the ancient slanting window sills.

It was so quiet. As the huge oak door closed behind us, we felt cocooned in a time warp. My spiritual antennae were picking up a tremendous sense of prayer in this place. We walked slowly up the tiny aisle, looking at the large wooden carvings on the walls, depicting the Ten Commandments in the language of a bygone age.

At the rear of the church, on a tiny balcony, stood the organ, which suddenly burst into husky song as the organist limbered the aging pipes into some sort of order, in preparation for the service. The large door opened again, briefly letting in a shaft of brilliant sunlight, and four or five other worshippers entered and sat down behind us.

The vicar, who had a very lovely, serene smile,

appeared from behind a curtain at the back of the church. "Hullo," he whispered. "It's nice to see you."

"Thank you," I replied. "It's wonderful to be here."

Adrian guided me to a pew at the very front of the church on the right-hand side. On the left, there was a special enclosed area which was set aside for the Lord of the Manor, in whose grounds the church was set. "We only sit there if we are invited to do so," Adrian explained.

The first hymn was introduced, and having been used to modern choruses, I found it difficult to cope with the ancient language and the taxing rhythms of the music itself. Adrian's beautiful voice thankfully covered all my mistakes, and we settled down to follow the service in the prayer book.

As we warbled our way through the Psalms and Canticles, I felt like the proverbial fish out of water. Did people really understand all these words? Adrian looked across and smiled. I raised my eyebrows and warbled on, to the best of my ability, trying not to get too embarrassed when I was singing a completely different tune from everyone else.

By the end of the service, when we had taken Communion at the ancient altar rail, and played "excuse me" as we passed the other communicants in the narrow aisle, I felt that it had been quite a spiritual exercise, one way and another. I missed the freedom to sing with my hands raised, and to dance around, should that seem the right thing to do. Here, I was being introduced to a much quieter, more reflective form of worship in which, once past the confines of the Book of Common Prayer, one entered into a hushed, expectant plane, far from the madding crowd of the nearby M25 motorway, and the endless stream of aircraft passing closely overhead on their final approach into Heathrow Airport, only twelve miles away.

As we left the church, we walked out into the warm summer sunshine, along the tree-lined lane, and then turned left towards the centre, a couple of hundred metres away. Adrian was on duty again, and he asked me if I would like to stay around to help with the children. I didn't know what to expect, but agreed to stay, determined to put the embarrassing comments of the Eton boys out of my mind each time I bumped into one of them.

The day passed so quickly with games of hide-and-seek in the main house, followed by a game of rounders in the grounds which was played with wet sponges, so that by the end everyone was soaked through. The children were great – so full of energy and enthusiasm. For most, this was their first holiday away from the busy streets of the inner cities, and this beautiful place was an oasis and a refuge. The boys from the College were also great, and worked very hard to keep their charges occupied and out of trouble.

Throughout it all, I watched Adrian as he dealt with the many and varied demands which were made on him. He seemed to have an amazing gift of talking to the children so that those who were shy became more confident, and those who were boisterous quietened down and listened. I just followed Adrian's lead, and was soon in the thick of all the action, running around the grounds with many eager hands clutching at mine.

By seven o'clock, I felt as though I had completed a double shift on the wards, and Adrian decided that the time had come to quieten things down a little, so he put on a video, and we all watched the film with drooping eyelids. A couple of children fell asleep where they sat, and Adrian and one of the other helpers carried them up to bed. The remainder had to make it upstairs under their own steam, and the communal bathrooms were soon filled with the sound of tired and quarrelsome voices as each child elbowed his or her way through the rest in order to clean their teeth.

A few minutes later, the children had changed into pyjamas and the lights were turned out. There was the odd squabble coming from the dormitories as one or two of the children decided that they really must settle old scores, and then there was peace. The rest of us staggered downstairs and collapsed in the armchairs in the spacious living room.

"How do you do this for a week at a time?" I asked Adrian as he sat down beside me.

"You just get on a roll, I suppose. It's when the children have gone home again that it really hits you, and then you feel that you could sleep for a week."

"Thank God they're going home tomorrow," groaned one of the helpers.

"The first night is usually the worst," Adrian continued. "That's because the children are so excited, and they can be up and about for most of the night. The second day, everyone is usually grumpy and short-tempered, so we go out on various outings to the ice rink, the zoo, the safari park – places like that."

I could see why the children had flourished. This holiday was providing them with so many new and exciting experiences, as well as the quiet and refined beauty of this wonderful house. It must have been such a contrast from the high-rise constrictions of the inner cities.

The next day, Adrian asked if I would like to accompany the group as he drove the children home in

150

the centre's minibus. It was a glorious day, and we drove into London, dodging the cut-throat traffic, and threading our way through the reams of traffic lights, roundabouts and bad-tempered motorists.

We eventually arrived at Hackney Town Hall, where there was a large group of mums, dads, brothers and sisters waiting to greet their children. As they left the minibus, they were embraced by many loving arms, and there were a few minutes of hugs and tearful good-byes as the children turned away and headed back to their homes. As they walked away, they were telling their families about all the exciting things they had seen and done, and as the last child was collected the world suddenly seemed a far quieter place.

I looked across at Adrian, whose face was pale, and the large, tell-tale dark rings under his eyes seemed to be increasing in size by the minute. "Are you alright?" I asked.

"I will be, when we get home," he said.

We made our way back to Dorney and put the ket-tle on for a coffee, which we drank, revelling in the peace and tranquillity which had now descended upon the centre. As we sat in Adrian's living room, Cleo, his cat, was eyeing up my toes with the intention of cap-turing one of them, which would no doubt provide a tasty morsel for later on. Downstairs, Gillian the house-keeper was busily working her way through 20 sets of bedding. Outside, we could hear the birds singing in the hedgerows, and overhead we could hear the aircraft as they approached Heathrow.

Then, for a few minutes, we fell asleep, with the summer sunshine streaming through the windows, and the fragrance of freshly cut grass wafting in from the grounds. In the distance, we could hear the sound of giant sprinklers which irrigated the farmer's fields all around. A lazy bee flew into the room briefly, and then decided that life was much more fun outside. I had to disagree. I couldn't think of anywhere that I would rather be.

Chapter Fifteen

The following few weeks passed in a blur of twirling rubber on tarmac as Adrian and I took it in turns to drive the 45 miles of the M25 and M4 motorways as we took every possible opportunity to be together. It was strange how everything in life seemed to take on a much more positive perspective. Things somehow seemed more balanced. Although work continued to be demanding and very tiring, it was all much more bearable now that my heart had found its home.

Six weeks after our first date, we were sitting in Adrian's living room when he suddenly said, "Where do you think this relationship is going, Hil?"

I was roused from my dozy stupor. Throughout the previous weeks, I had made a vow to myself that I wouldn't say anything about the night of the May ball. In no way did I want to pressurise Adrian. If this relationship was meant to be, then it had to be right for him, absolutely. But now that I was put on the spot like this, I felt that I should tell him about what had happened that night.

I took a deep breath. "Well," I said, trying very hard to keep a straight face. "You know the May ball?"

"Of course," he replied.

"Well. That night, after everyone had gone home, I

had a strange feeling that the Lord was trying to tell me something."

"And what was that?"

"You'll never believe this."

"Try me. Go on, I'm intrigued now!"

"Well. Oh dear, this all sounds very silly now. I hope you won't be cross."

"Come on! I can't bear the suspense!"

"Well."

"Stop saying 'Well'!"

"I believe He said ... Are you sure you want to hear this?"

"Ahhhhh!" I took that as a "Yes".

"I believe He said that we were supposed to get married." There was a momentary pause, and I sat searching his face for some sort of response. A second later, he was down on the floor, on one knee.

"Well, that's it, then," he said. "Hil, will you marry me?"

"Of course I will!"

We put the kettle on, and tried to decide when would be the best time for the wedding. The lease on the house in Welwyn Garden City was due to expire at the end of the following May, so it seemed like a good idea to arrange the wedding for the final Saturday in the month. This would give us about six months in which to arrange the whole thing. Easy, really.

The following few weeks were a whirlwind of travelling back and forth and making arrangements. It was a time of making new relationships with Adrian's family and, having met them, I began to understand why Adrian was such a lovely person.

I successfully applied for a midwifery post at Wexham Park Hospital in Slough, to begin work there two weeks after the wedding. I continued to work and live in Welwyn until three days before the big day. We were determined not to live together before our wedding, because we wanted it to be the beginning of something very special. The price of this was sometimes quite high, and some evenings either Adrian or I would end up driving back to our respective homes very late at night.

On one particular night, there was very dense fog, the worst I had ever encountered, and I had to drive home because I was due at work at 7:30 the following morning. I set out gingerly along the winding roads leading to the M4, and the fog was patchy, but I felt confident to drive. On the motorway, however, it seemed to suddenly descend, and I could hardly see the lorry which was only a few feet in front of me.

The journey, which would normally have taken about an hour, took three, and by the time I arrived home, it was one o'clock and I was completely exhausted. The following shift was, needless to say, far from easy.

Those six months, in one sense, passed very quickly, and there never seemed to be a moment to stop and draw breath. In another sense, though, the time could not pass quickly enough. We found it difficult to be apart for long, and couldn't wait until we could finally set up home together.

During my final week at work in Welwyn, I was allocated to the Delivery Suite, which was normally my preference anyway, but on my penultimate day, I was given a case which has haunted me to this day. I was handed the notes of a young woman whose baby had died some five days previously *in utero*, and whose labour was being induced in order to remove the baby.

The pregnancy had gone to full term, and it was only a routine scan which had made the grim discovery, after the mother had noticed a sudden lack of movement from the baby inside her.

I had never cared for anyone in this situation before, and I battled hard with my own feelings of sorrow for this lovely young woman, Karen, and her husband Trevor. Childbirth is usually a tremendously positive life event, but this woman's ordeal had absolutely nothing that could be said to be positive about it. Karen was going to have to endure all the pain with nothing but emptiness at the end of it. I felt deeply saddened for her, but had to put my own feelings aside and do the best I could to encourage her, and lessen her pain.

When I entered the room, I was immediately struck by the eerie quietness. A delivery room is usually filled with the melodic thumping of the baby's heart from the cardiac monitor, and the sound of paper rolling imperceptibly forward, revealing a trace of the baby's heart rate in relation to the mother's contractions. But, in this case, there was none of that. There was just Karen, lying quietly on her side, whilst Trevor stroked her hand, and kissed her gently. I knew that this room was the last place in the entire world that they wanted to be. It was my job to make the ordeal as bearable as possible.

The evening shift wore on, and Karen's labour was long and arduous. I kept increasing the syntocinon drip to maintain the uterine contractions, but by the end of the shift, Karen had only progressed to four centimetres in dilatation. She still had a way to go before this baby would escape from the hidden recesses of her womb.

I felt guilty as I handed her care over to the night staff. It was such a relief not to have had to deal with the delivery itself, and I felt sure that the baby would be born during the night. I knew that all the staff on duty that night were very experienced midwives, and I felt sure that they would handle the situation far better than I could, anyway.

The following morning, I was sent around to Delivery Suite once again and, to my horror, discovered that Karen was still there, and that she was still in labour. My heart went out to her. She must have had a most terrible night, with little or no sleep, and the constant pain of a labour which never seemed to end.

I approached her room with trepidation. I knew that this would be my last delivery in this hospital, and felt ill-prepared to handle the situation expertly. But, we did our best, and by administering adequate analgesia, and encouraging Karen to relax as much as possible, we eventually came to the point where she could finally begin to push her little child out into the world.

It was about eleven o'clock. Trevor was grey with fatigue, but he roused himself heroically to help Karen find a more comfortable position in which she could most effectively push.

An hour passed, and still there was little progress. Half an hour later, and I could just about see the tip of the baby's head. Fifteen minutes later, and the head was beginning to "crown", which meant that it would soon be free from the birth canal.

I began to flex the baby's head, and inwardly recoiled as the skull bones grated over one another in my hands. Although I was wearing a face mask, the odour emanating from the baby's flesh, and the amniotic fluid surrounding it, was putrid. I wondered how this was affecting Karen and Trevor but they were locked into their part of playing this tragedy out to its bitter conclusion.

"Another little push, Karen. That's brilliant. You're doing so well." How many times had I used these words, but never in a situation like this. A couple of pushes later, and the baby's head was born. The majority of babies are born with their faces turned downwards, towards the bed, but this little child was facing upwards, towards me. I stared in horror at her sunken features, and felt my hands tremble as I tried to apply traction to rotate her body to deliver the shoulders. I felt that if I pulled with much force, then the head would very easily come off in my hands.

With thumping heart, I gently and very slowly eased the head and neck around, and with a giant effort from Karen, the baby's body eventually was born. Instinctively, I placed the baby quickly onto the sterile green towels between Karen's legs, and half covered the baby's face. I had never seen anything so ghastly in all my life, and I wanted to protect Karen and Trevor.

I tried to deliver the placenta, but the umbilical cord was also disintegrating, and I had to wait and very slowly apply traction before this final part of the delivery was complete. Madge, one of the staff midwives, had entered the room to clean up the baby so that the parents could hold her, and I was thankful for her maturity, and her ability to handle the little body. To my horror, I found that, having delivered the little child, I could not bring myself to touch her again.

Madge very tenderly wrapped the little body in a pretty pink blanket, and handed her to Karen. I flinched, and then, to my utter amazement, she cuddled the little baby to her heart, and smiled at Trevor. "Isn't she beautiful?" she said.

I bundled the remaining debris from the delivery onto the trolley, and excused myself from the room. As the door closed behind me, the first gulping sobs erupted. I tried with every ounce of strength to suppress them, and walked quickly into a sluice as far away from the delivery room as was possible. But it was no good, and I washed the delivery instruments, crashing them around in an effort to disguise the sobs which were so loud and embarrassing. I felt like a child who had been reprimanded. I didn't know how to cope with this situation, which was completely out of my control.

I returned to the office, and began to write up the delivery notes, but the sobs would not submit to social niceties. I persevered, and then Sister Dunlop entered the room.

"Hilary, you must take a break," she said. "You can't write up your notes like that. Come on, love. We'll make you a cup of tea. Come on, love, come and sit down, away from all this."

She took me to a spare room at the far end of the unit, and Jayne, the auxiliary nurse, arrived with a pot of tea and a cup and saucer. I was highly honoured. Saucers were only used for special occasions. A few minutes later, one of the senior midwives entered the room.

"I heard what happened, Hilary."

"I'm really sorry, but I just couldn't ... " I could feel the tears ganging up again.

"It's not really surprising. You're getting married on Saturday, for heaven's sake. In retrospect, I think that it was very unfair that this case was allocated to you when you've so much happening in your private life."

I was immensely touched by her kindness, and I finally managed to complete the notes, and then took my lunch break. During this time, I walked up and down the familiar corridors, taking in the views from the windows on the fifth floor. How many times had I marched up and down here, on some urgent mission or other, and yet had never really taken the time to see what was all around?

As I looked out over the car park, my eye was caught by numerous objects either dangling from, or floating just above, my car. I did a double take and looked again, and saw several of my colleagues beavering busily around it. One was draping a full roll of toilet tissue over every available aspect, and another was inflating sterile gloves and tying them with string to the bumper and wing mirrors. A third was spraying a huge heart of foam over the windscreen. I found myself laughing in spite of the morning's events.

I sat down in the empty staff room, and thought about how much I was going to miss this place. There were some wonderful people here, and in spite of all the traumas, worries and demands, I had truly found my niche here, and it was going to be a real wrench to leave it.

A few minutes later, the three who had conspired to deck my car came into the room. They were laughing and stuffing cans of foam into plastic bags. When they saw that I was in the room, they immediately pretended to be casual, as though nothing had happened. The decoration of the car was meant to be a surprise, so I played along with them, and pretended that I hadn't noticed it at all.

Then Sister Ruby and all the midwives on my team came in, and presented me with wedding gifts. I wished that Adrian was there to see the love and generosity of these wonderful people with whom I had been so privileged to work.

Before leaving the unit, I returned to the room where Karen and Trevor had spent the previous 24 hours. Karen was awaiting transfer back to the antenatal ward, where she could rest without the sound of crying babies. She looked exhausted, and Trevor's eyes were also ringed with the dark circles of the insomniac. Their eyes were red, and freshly washed with a multitude of tears. The baby, whom they had called Charlotte, was lying in a little cot next to the delivery bed. As I entered the room, I could feel that my own tears were frighteningly near the surface, too.

"I'm so very sorry," I began.

"Thank you so much for all you did." Karen held her hand out to me. I squeezed it, and then leant forward and embraced her, trying to express the sadness and support which were impossible to convey with mere words. I could say no more. Then Trevor handed me a little basket of silk flowers.

"These are for you," he said. "We hope that you will think of us every time you look at them."

I nodded, and tried to smile. I tried to speak, but only a strangled croak came out in the place of the calm, professional voice that I was attempting to find.

"Thank you so much. I must go now. Please take care ... "

I turned and left the room, and in doing so, felt as though a chapter of my life was closing behind me. I wondered why this had had to be my last delivery. Why should four years of intense study, hard work and commitment end in such tragedy? How would Karen and Trevor move on from this? As I walked down the stairs to the basement in order to get changed, I silently prayed for them.

Once changed, I handed back my supply of uniforms to the sewing department, and returned my locker key. All the material aspects of belonging were quietly being relinquished. I walked up to the ground floor, and the bright sunlight was dazzling. To my amazement, most of the staff from my team were waiting for me. I could see the balloons and toilet tissue on my car blowing enthusiastically in the breeze.

"We thought we'd see you off the premises, just in case you changed your mind!"

We walked out to the car park, and then in a moment of sheer devilment, I casually walked up to the car which was parked next to mine, and put my key to its lock. I waited for a couple of seconds, and then looked up. I wished that this moment could have been captured on film; their faces were a picture – for a terrible moment, they thought that they had decorated the wrong car!

"Only kidding!" I said, and we all laughed and hugged.

"You know you've got to drive it all the way around the car park, now!" So I did, waving and hooting the horn. I stopped short of driving it home as it was, however. After half an hour spent untying the inflated gloves, green aprons, toilet tissue, etc., the car was finally roadworthy once again.

It was only when I arrived home that I realised why I had been getting strange looks from motorists driving in the opposite direction. I had forgotten to take off two rather suggestive balloons which were tied to the radiator grille at the front!

It felt strange coming back to the house, which was empty at that time. Janine and Linda were still at work, and this house, which was full of memories and laughter, now felt like a shell which I was about to discard, in preparation for moving on. I went to my room and lay down on the bed. I was so tired. It had been an exhausting day, and all I wanted to do was sleep. But my mind was whirring with an endless list of things which still needed to be done, including the small matter of packing up all my belongings, once again.

I fell asleep to the sound of birds singing in the late spring sunshine, and the ticking of my little red clock at the side of the bed.

Chapter Sixteen

The following afternoon, Adrian arrived at the house with the minibus from the conference centre. Together, we packed almost all my worldly possessions into it, including an old bicycle which had been given to me at Christmas when I was eleven years old. My mum had manhandled it into my bedroom at midnight on Christmas Eve, and the last vestiges of my belief in Father Christmas had evaporated with the accidental ringing of the bicycle's bell.

I left my wedding dress, veil and a sleeping bag at the house with the intention of returning the following evening for the quietest hen night on record.

We spent Wednesday afternoon unpacking everything, and trying to find room for my clothes in Adrian's two-bedroomed flat. Over the previous few months, we had been working together to make it into a home. Where Adrian had used shirts hanging from the curtain rails to block out the light, we now had pretty drapes which matched the décor of each room. It was beginning to look more like home.

When we had had enough of the nest-building, we went for a walk by the river. We watched the Eton boys as they rowed up the Thames, wearing straw boaters filled with flowers. Then, on command, they stood up in their narrow boats, raised their hats, and the flowers fell in cascades into the gently flowing waters. This was accompanied by a loud cheer, which seemed to echo the mood of our own hearts. We had nearly made it to our own Big Day.

I spent that night at the flat, and Adrian slept on the floor in the living room. He was truly looking forward to the time when he wouldn't be banished there every night! The following afternoon, I drove back to Welwyn and spent a very gentle evening with Janine and Linda. It felt strange, and I felt guilty to be leaving them, and we talked about the previous year in which so much had happened.

Janine had also become engaged, and was looking forward to her own wedding in six weeks' time. Linda was busily contemplating a new job, and looking forward to that with excitement. In the meantime, however, they were both preparing for their role as bridesmaids in two days' time.

We sat drinking a bottle of wine whilst the late sunshine poured through the patio windows. "You'll be fine, Hil – I only wish that it was our wedding on Saturday." Janine was sitting on the arm of a chair, whilst Mark, her fiancé, sat in the chair, gently stroking her leg. I kept thinking of how Linda must be feeling. In the past, I had struggled with jealousy on a grand scale if one of my friends was getting married.

It was stupid, I knew, but it was something about which I seemed to have little control, and it was the source of considerable remorse. In the months before moving in with Janine and Linda, a friend from the Hospital Christian Fellowship had been married to a handsome man whom she had met at her local church. I had been invited to the wedding, but found it very difficult when at the reception, he had picked her up and swirled her around the room, dancing to "Cherish the Love we Have".

I had felt gutted, lonely, frustrated, angry, jealous ... you name all the negative emotions, and I'd embraced them all. Why didn't anyone love me? I was trying so hard to live an honest, good life. I had just about reached the point of acceptance that marriage might not be God's plan for me. Then the May ball changed everything.

I thought back to the ways in which the Lord had worked through every situation. From the demoralising situation in the Nurses' Home, to the tea where I'd first met Janine, the friendship which Adrian and Janine had shared, and our meeting at the house. Also I recalled the words of the Bible which had encouraged me to move there in the first place. It was all a jigsaw, which was finally culminating in this, our marriage.

The Thursday night was filled with excited dreams about wedding bells, and wondering whether the beautiful weather would hold for the photographs on Saturday. I rolled around uncomfortably in the sleeping bag, and was awake as the first light of dawn crept across the sky at four o'clock in the morning. *This is the day*, I thought to myself, *that I leave this place for ever. Today, I am going to move to the home of the one I love.* And tomorrow, well, it couldn't come quickly enough.

I left the house mid-morning, carrying my wedding dress which was wrapped in a sheet. I placed it gently on the back seat, and locking the house door for the last time, I bent down and posted the keys through the letter box. As I let go of the keys, it was as though I was letting go of the past, and turning to face a new and exciting future.

The car seemed to drive itself to Dorney. It had

done the journey often enough, and it didn't seem long before I was swinging the Cortina into the gravel drive at the centre. There was a very definite feeling of "coming home".

That afternoon, Adrian's mum and sister decorated the church with flowers. I was so glad that they had offered to do this, because in all the busy-ness I had completely forgotten that the church would need to be prepared too. A couple of Adrian's brothers were also there, together with Adrian's assistant, Elizabeth, who was now the girlfriend of Adrian's best man, Steve. Together with Sam and Theresa, who performed most of the centre's domestic duties, it made quite a large gathering. There was a real air of expectancy, as everyone prepared their best clothes for the following day. I felt humbled and grateful that so many people had gone to so much trouble for us.

Adrian was still recovering from the after-effects of his stag night. Steve had taken him to several pubs, and together with some friends, they had drunk a fair few pints and chasers. In the early hours of Friday morning, Adrian had been up with the larks, shouting for "Ralph" and "Huey" into the toilet's unsympathetic bowl. Jon, one of his friends, had then taken him out for a walk in the early morning air to try to clear his head a little more.

I spent the night in the single bed in Adrian's room. The previous day, we had manhandled the double bed into position in readiness for our return from honeymoon. There was even a story behind the bed itself. It had belonged to the previous Bishop of Buckingham, who had approached the conference centre, offering it to anyone who might have use of it. In fact, it had just arrived before my first visit to Dorney, and one of the first things Adrian had said to me then was "Do you know anyone who needs a double bed?"

I had inwardly giggled to myself, because I knew that, if I had heard the Lord correctly, then, at some time in the future, we might well be needing it ourselves. At the time, however, I had simply answered, "No, not at the moment." And left it at that.

At eight o'clock on Saturday morning, I was up and singing, and fighting a spirited battle with the new king-size duvet and its cover. Nobody ever tells you that these things have a mind of their own, and a cunning plan to envelop you alive. I continued to stuff the duvet into its cover until I realised that it was all the wrong way around, and had to start again. Eventually, it admitted defeat, and sat there, sulking in a squashed-looking manner on a freshly made bed.

I felt a pang of nervousness. After all these months spent waiting for the culmination of our physical relationship, I suddenly felt terrified. Supposing I was a disappointment to Adrian? I sat looking glumly at the bed, wondering if it would be friend or foe. It was too late now. We would just have to see.

I ate a bowl of muesli, enjoying the sound of the birdsong in the surrounding trees. This was such a peaceful place when it wasn't full of visitors. I went down to the breakfast room in the main house, and tried to paint my fingernails, whilst talking to Elizabeth.

"You're up early," she said. "Are you nervous?"

"Yes and no," I replied. "My hands are shaking, and the nail polish is going everywhere, so it's probably more yes than no."

A little while later, Adrian arrived back from Steve's flat. We had deliberately decided to break with

169

the tradition of not seeing each other before the wedding, and we walked slowly down the lane towards the church. We wanted to go there before all the other guests arrived, so that we could commit our wedding, and our marriage, to God. We wanted Jesus to be central, not only to this day, but to the rest of our lives together.

We walked down the leafy lane, and the sunshine held that humid sort of heat which you know will precede a storm. I kept looking up at the sky, and watched the clouds as they continued to build. As we entered the church, it was sublimely peaceful. The atmosphere was dark and womb-like, but bright specks of dust danced ever higher in the shafts of sunlight which poured through the windows on the eastern aspect of the building. The altar itself was draped in sunlight. We sat down together and prayed.

We thanked the Lord for bringing us together, and for this day, in which we prayed that He would be central. We prayed for all our guests that they might experience some of His love and blessing. After about 20 minutes, we left the church and headed back to the centre.

Janine had just arrived, and together we headed into Burnham to have our hair cut. It was great to be pampered, but I kept watching the clock, and wondered how our guests were coping with their journeys. Adrian had friends and family who were travelling large distances, and some of my friends were coming from work, together with some members of my family. I only hoped that they were better at following directions than I was.

It was almost midday by the time we had finished at the salon, and we arrived back at Dorney just as my sister Irene and her husband Bob were pulling into the drive.

"Hullo, Hilly darling, how lovely to see you! How's it all going?"

"Fine, thank you. Well, I hope so, anyway."

"We've brought plenty of bubbly to wet your whistle before you go to the church." I think a look of dismay must have crossed my face at this point. I wasn't used to drinking in the afternoon, and I didn't want to go swaying down the aisle under the influence!

"Don't worry about a thing, darling. Big sister is here now, and I've brought all my make-up kit with me. You're going to look like a princess."

So, under Irene's sisterly wing, I was wafted up the stairs to the flat. Adrian's mum, Dorothy, came through the other entrance from the main house, just as Bob placed four bottles of champagne in a sink full of cold water. "Some of your friends from work have arrived, Hilary. Would you like to come and greet them?"

We all went downstairs, and I introduced Irene and Bob to Adrian's family, and then to my friends. We all sat down and chatted about journeys, the weather, work, anything and everything. I kept watching the clock. The wedding was due to begin at 3:30, and the photographer was due to arrive an hour prior to that. We needed to have lunch, and then I would need to have another bath and get dressed ... And outside, the clouds were gathering in size and number. If only the rain would hold off until after the photos. I didn't mind what happened after that.

Lunch consisted of pizza washed down with champagne. I'm not sure that gourmets would recommend such a combination, but it hit the spot. Irene kept commenting on how calm I was. I tried to explain that I was calm because I knew that Adrian was the man for me. Somewhere amongst all the swirling practicalities, there

171

was a part of me which was serene and at peace. Adrian was a wonderful man, and I knew that I loved him completely, and without a doubt. I felt sure that God had brought us together for a purpose, and that this day was the beginning of a real adventure.

Lunch over, I retreated to the bathroom for a leisurely soak. It was the only place where people did not continually ask me for something or another. I had just come out of the bath when mum arrived from my parents' new home in Hertfordshire. It was so good to see her. At last I felt that things were all coming together. My father was not able to come to the wedding. I was sad that he was going to miss out on a really special day. Bob had very kindly agreed to give me away, and for that, I was very grateful.

Irene performed wonders with her make-up kit, and just after I had put on the dress, and everyone had wanted to inspect my very unimpressive underwear, the photographer arrived. Janine, Linda and I posed for photos in the living room. Throughout the main house, the dormitories were full of guests changing into their best togs. I could hear many excited voices and a lot of laughter. It was wonderful.

The minute hand seemed to be on a go-slow, and sluggishly wound its way around the clock's face. At 3:10, the guests began to walk off down the lane towards the church. At 3:20, the chauffeur drove Janine and Linda to the church, leaving Bob and I twiddling our thumbs.

At 3:25 I could bear the suspense no longer, and made my way down the main stairway in the house. I walked into the living room where I would be able to see the white Mercedes when it arrived. I was surprised to see Fred, the husband of the centre's housekeeper,

Nellie, sitting in the quietness. I had forgotten that he had agreed to house-sit for us, to deter any possible thieves. Adrian's first wedding ring had already been stolen from his flat, and we didn't want anything else to go missing.

"How are you, Fred?"

"Oh, you know, fair to middling."

"Thank you so much for looking after the house for us; we really appreciate it."

"That's alright. Aren't you cutting it a bit fine to get to the church?"

"I think the chauffeur wants to make me late."

He grinned wryly. "That's a woman's prerogative, isn't it?"

I was just about to agree when the car, bedecked with pink ribbons, turned into the drive. "Come on, Hilly, your chariot awaits." Bob was laughing quietly. I think that I must have looked annoyed when the chauffeur eventually climbed out of the car, because he quickly apologised for being late.

"Never mind, as long as we get there soon." I grabbed armfuls of copious skirts, together with the full-length veil and bouquet, and folded myself carefully into the car. Bob sat on the other side, and we began our one-and-a-half-minute journey to the church.

The warm air was filled with the sound of the bells ringing from the ancient bell tower. As we turned slowly into the church's tiny forecourt, I could feel the butterflies multiplying by the second. As the car came to a standstill, I leapt out, without waiting for the chauffeur to open the door. I was determined to do away with all the traditions, and I wanted this wedding to go ahead before it started to rain. Janine and Linda were waiting at the gate, and they looked beautiful. We posed for a couple of photos, and then walked up to the porch, where Colin, our vicar, was patiently waiting.

I could hear the organ playing asthmatically and, as Colin gave John, the organist, the nod, the bridal march started up. We had chosen the theme music to *Chariots of Fire*, which was very meaningful to us both. That film tells the story of the athlete Eric Liddle. He was a Christian who refused to take part in the Olympic games if it meant that he had to run on a Sunday. He had been put under tremendous pressure from the highest authorities to change his mind, but he would not, and had to run in another race. I had been so impressed with his courage and determination, and also the fact that he acknowledged that all of his gifts came from God anyway.

It was at this point that I dearly wished that Adrian and I had been able to take part in a wedding rehearsal. "You'll be fine, I'm sure," Colin had said. "You'll know what to do."

Now, *Chariots of Fire* has a long introduction before the main piece of the music begins, and the aisle at the church is extremely short so, when Colin started to process up the aisle, I grabbed his arm, and whispered loudly, "No! Not yet!"

He turned around and smiled benignly. "Perhaps you'll let me know when we can start walking?" He was obviously experienced at dealing with stroppy brides! The introduction continued, and we finally came to the point where we could begin. I nudged Colin, who obligingly walked slowly forward, and then turned right.

Adrian's friends were sitting on the right, and everyone was smiling. On the left were my friends, some of whom gave me a little wave as we walked slowly by. It was only when I reached Adrian that I realised that our families had been seated in the choir stalls, and that we would have to say our vows whilst facing them all. It was at this point that the adrenalin started to flow in abundance. I reached for Adrian's hand, and we clung to each other for dear life. There was no turning back.

We began to sing, and the nerves steadied a bit as we found our voices. Concentrating on the words to the hymn, "And Can it Be?", really helped, especially when it came to the words, "My chains fell off, my heart was free, I rose, went forth and followed Thee". It had become a joke in Adrian's family that the words should be amended to: "My chains fell off, my bike free-wheeled, I rose, went forth, and hit a tree". We were all giggling by this time, which did wonders to break the ice.

As we continued through the service, several spelling errors on the Order of Service gave rise to fur-ther hilarity. The Holy Spirit was now called Spirity, and several other mistakes only seemed to emphasise the fact that this really was not a high-society wedding at all. Doubtless, through the generations, many noble men and women had been married in this ancient place, and we knew that many very successful couples contin-ued the tradition in this tiny country church, but we were different. We were neither of noble birth, nor were we nouveau riche – we were just here, trying to follow God, wherever He chose to lead us.

Colin spoke for a few minutes about the importance of honouring God, of trying to treat one another with respect, and honouring the vows which we were about to make. Then, facing one another, we made promises to one another, knowing full well that we would need the Lord's help if we were truly to upkeep them.

With trembling hands, we exchanged rings, and moved forward to the altar where we knelt and Colin prayed a blessing upon our union. In spite of all the wonderful solemnity of the occasion, the nagging thought which kept going through my mind was that of a more practical nature. Would my skirt hoop behave itself as I knelt down?

When I was six years old, my mum had taken me to audition for a part in the production of *The King and I*, at the Palace Theatre, Watford. It had entailed six months of weekly rehearsals, and when it came to the dress rehearsals, some of the young ladies had the most awful trouble with the hoops on their enormous skirts. Every time they had to kneel down, some of the skirts would shoot up at the back, revealing all underneath. My sister, Alison, and I had giggled helplessly every time this happened, and it had left an indelible memory, which was now reactivated.

Consequently, I knelt down very carefully, and thought that all was going well until, halfway through the prayer, I heard a tiny crack. Adrian heard it too, and looked across anxiously. I smiled at him, and tried to look reassuring. The plastic hoop had managed to wriggle free from its linen support, and was sticking out at a jaunty angle. I knew it couldn't be trusted. There was nothing I could do about it now, and at least the skirt wasn't flying up in the air. I had to be thankful for small mercies!

When we moved into the side chapel to sign the register, Linda and Janine performed running repairs on the hoop, and finally emerged from the mountain of petticoats giving me the thumbs up. We walked down the aisle to a rather breathless rendition of Handel's "Arrival of the Queen of Sheba", and stepped outside to find, rather miraculously, that the sun was still shining.

We filed around the back of the church and stood

176

next to its ancient walls whilst everyone took photos, and Adrian and I felt like royalty. The sun was beating down, and we could feel its rays penetrating our backs with its moist heat. My friends from work all looked very grand in their hats and high heels, and they were eyeing up one of the other guests whose baby was due within the next few weeks. At least, if anything happened, I knew she would be in good hands.

We were finally able to leave the grounds, and returned to the Mercedes. The chauffeur was at the ready this time, and I didn't have to open the door myself. A few more photos were taken, and then we were on our way, across Dorney Common to Eton Wick Village Hall where, we hoped, the caterers had everything under control.

After receiving our guests, we were entertained by Janine singing some beautiful worship songs, and then Adrian's brother, Richard, played "Annie's Song" on his flute. These were two beautiful and very touching wedding gifts which we have always treasured.

The buffet meal which followed was a blur of talking to various people, and asking Steve to kindly remove the leg of his chair from my veil, as every time he moved, it became stuck underneath the chair. As the veil was still firmly applied to my head at the time, the result was a small amount of hair loss, and a rather crooked flower arrangement.

We were soon dancing the evening away, and then it was time for us to leave. Adrian and I changed quickly, and walked down the long rows of guests, hugging and kissing each in turn. We were just about to make our grand exit when I suddenly realised that I'd left my handbag at the other end of the room, and had to repeat the hugging and kissing over again.

We walked out of the hall, and for the first time noticed the rain which was coming down in sheets. Adrian's Marina had been decked out in the finest lager tins and toilet tissue, and the latter lay rather limply over almost the entire surface of the car. We drove back over the common with the sound of cans jangling and scraping over the cattle grids. We rushed up to the flat, grabbed our suitcases, and then placed them in the boot of the Cortina. We were not going to drive all the way to Hampshire with the cans bouncing behind us! We would sort out the Marina when we returned from honeymoon. And then we were off. My mind was still whirling with lists of things that I hoped that I had remembered.

We drove on in silence. "Are you alright, Adrain?" He had become used to this rather odd pronunciation of his name.

"I'm alright; are you?"

"I'm fine, don't worry." Silence for a few minutes. "It was wonderful to see all my friends from work. I'm so glad that they came."

"You've got some lovely friends, Hil."

"Can you remember that piece of music we were dancing to when I got cramp? You know the one; it had violins in it." I tried to mimic the tune but failed miserably. After a few minutes of recollection, we finally came to the conclusion that the song was "Come on, Eileen" by Dexy's Midnight Runners. The rest of the journey we tried to remember some of the words, but we didn't do too well with that, either.

After about an hour, we arrived in Alton, at the Swan Inn. Adrian carried the suitcases up to our room, which was beautiful, with an en suite bathroom, and a complimentary bottle of champagne. We both suddenly felt rather shy, so I decided to have another bath, the third of the day.

Adrian waited patiently, and when I eventually emerged, he had the champagne at the ready. We drank one glass, and then, deciding that Dutch courage might be a good idea under the circumstances, we drank another, and then set about the task of getting to know each other a little better.

Chapter Seventeen

The following day, we made our way to Bransgore, on the edge of the New Forest, where Colin, our vicar, had offered us the use of his holiday home. When we arrived, we found a bottle of wine with two glasses waiting in the living room.

We dragged the suitcases into the house. They were still scattering the confetti which Adrian's sister Hazel had placed inside them. We had certainly made our mark at the hotel when we first opened the cases and half a ton of the stuff had flung itself everywhere! We had tried to clear it up, but it was a job which definitely needed the help of a vacuum cleaner, which was one of the few things we hadn't remembered to bring.

We were absolutely exhausted, so we made a cup of coffee and collapsed in the living room for a while. It felt really strange. We were married, and yet we still had so much to learn about one another. We hadn't made any definite plans for our honeymoon; all that we really wanted was to be together, alone, and far away from the distractions and demands of our work.

The busy-ness of the past few months seemed to catch up with us, and to counterbalance the highs of the previous few days, we both felt worn out beyond words. We had tried to trust God and not to worry about the wedding, but it had still taken its toll, as the demands of both of our jobs had been unrelenting. Consequently, we spent much of the first few days in bed, only venturing out to dine at a restaurant in the evenings.

We discovered a quaint little place called the Copper Skillet, and we became regular visitors there. We would sit and look at one another, and watch the world walk by as the early summer sunshine slanted through the window. We wondered how many other people here were on their honeymoon, and watched out for the tell-tale signs, smiling knowingly at couples who looked as soppy as we did.

One evening, we decided to take a walk by the sea following our meal. It was a blustery evening, and the wind coming off the sea had a definite chill to it. I decided to lock my handbag in the boot of the Cortina, rather than have it flopping and banging all over the place in the strong wind. We set off, and walked a fair distance on the sand. Adrian was enjoying skimming stones, and we searched for as many flat ones as we could find.

We must have walked for about an hour, and the wind and the fresh air had done wonders to revive our spirits. We returned to the car, and headed back to the house. It was only then that I remembered my handbag, and went back to the car to get it. I was horrified when I found that the boot was empty.

"I must have brought it into the house, Adrain. It's not in the car."

"It's not in the house, Hil. I've looked everywhere in here."

Then the dull, creeping coldness of realisation hit home. I'd been carrying over £100 in cash, with my savings book, together with a treasured ring which had been given to me in Hong Kong.

"It can't have gone, can it?"

"It looks that way, Hil."

I did the pathetic thing and started to cry, and then the thought came to me that Jesus had taught us not to enter into thoughts of retribution when someone does us wrong. He taught us that we should pray for those people, so Adrian and I sat down and began to pray for the person who had broken into our car and stolen my belongings. We prayed that they might be aware of what was right, and that God would make Himself known to them in a very real way.

Praying helped a bit, but I still felt the pain of losing things which were precious. Every time the feelings of injustice returned, I continued to pray for the person who had stolen the bag. It was a matter of trying to put Jesus's teaching into practice. It wasn't easy or comfortable, but there was a sense that this was the right thing to do. The next day, we informed the local police about the theft, and had to leave the situation in their hands.

Over the next few days, we continued to explore the Dorset coast, stopping to take walks, and admiring the beautiful countryside all around. We contacted a friend who lived on the Isle of Wight, and arranged to go across on the ferry. The only slight hitch in the preparations was when we had eaten a tandoori curry the previous night in Lyndhurst and the resulting intestinal hurry put our travel plans in question for a while. Thankfully, the effects were short-lived, and we did make it across to see Ali and her boyfriend Dick.

We ventured up in the chairlift, and marvelled as the views of the island spread out beneath us. It was magical and magnificent, even if somewhat alarming at times. We clung on tightly to the bar which was holding us into our seats, and gasped as the ground disappeared beneath our feet. We felt as though we were on top of a very wonderful world.

Later on in the day, we returned to the mainland, and steered clear of the Indian restaurant. I was still missing my handbag and its contents, but there was nothing we could do about it. It had gone, and we just had to accept the fact, and try to enjoy the remainder of the holiday.

All too soon, it was over, and we had to pack our things and head for home. It felt strange to be returning to Dorney as man and wife. We walked into the main house and found Colin and his wife Jen in the breakfast room. "Hullo," said Jen, "did you have a good time?"

"It was wonderful. Thank you so much for the use of your house – it is beautiful."

"It's funny, Hilary, but you look just the same as when you left. I expected you to look different, somehow."

I blushed. I felt different. Marriage had changed us. We were now two halves of a whole, joined in mind, body and spirit, and we would never be the same again. This was not to say that everything was going to be plain sailing, by any means.

A week or so after our return to Dorney, we had a most ridiculous argument about something, and Adrian rode away on a moped. I felt a mixture of anger, frustration and worry as he bounced and popped over the gravelly drive on this tiny machine. He looked so vulnerable, as he hung on grimly, taking the corners with as much panache as the little bike would allow. I couldn't help but notice the resemblance between Adrian and a match stick, as the helmet which he had crammed onto his head was a most attractive blue.

I went through the entire gamut of emotions in the hour he was away. Would he ever return? Had I blown it forever by being pig-headed and stubborn? Had he been pig-headed and stubborn? By the time Adrian finally returned, my stomach was in knots, and I was so relieved to see him, that all that had gone before was no longer of any relevance. I rushed down the back steps. "Are you alright? I'm so sorry that I was so stupid. Where did you go?"

He hopped off the bike, and we hugged each other tightly. "I'm sorry, Hil, I was just getting a bit fed up. I rode out to the hospital, and sat by the lake for a while. I hope you weren't too worried."

"I'm just really glad you're back." We came to the conclusion that marriage probably meant that we would end up getting annoyed from time to time, but as long as we both kept working at it, then we would stand a chance.

The following day, we had the most wonderful news. Adrian received a phone call from the police in Dorset. Against all the odds, my handbag had been found! Apparently, it had been discovered on the beach about seven miles away from where we had been walking. It was soiled by the sea water, but, miraculously, none of the contents had been taken. We had prayed that God would speak to the person who had stolen it, but we would never know exactly what had happened. We were so thankful that our prayers had been answered, and this timely encouragement from the Lord raised our spirits immensely.

We drove down the following day, and were amazed to find all the money and the ring still inside the bag. Apparently, a very honest walker had discovered it as she had been taking her daily constitutional

185

down by the sea shore. We thanked God for such an honest person, and prayed that she would also experience a tremendous blessing as a result.

Driving home, we had time to reflect on the past three weeks. We were making the transition between singleness and marriage. Adrian had been thrown right back into the thick of things at work with the onset of the childrens' summer holidays at the centre, and I had completed my first week at my new job.

It had felt very strange beginning work at Wexham Park. It was rather like the transition one makes from being in the top class at junior school to becoming a minnow in the first year at senior school. I had been shown around the various departments, and had worked for a shift in each area. My first shift had been on the Delivery Suite, and I had longed to be given the care of a young woman who was in established labour, but I was instructed to stand back and watch another midwife who was fully conversant with delivering babies "the Wexham Park way". I was very disappointed as I really needed to get back in the saddle, and deliver a live baby to lay to rest the ghosts which still haunted me from Welwyn.

It wasn't to be, however, and I was allocated a six-month placement in the antenatal clinic. The senior midwives had actually been very kind because they thought that the regular hours of the clinic would be most helpful to a newly married midwife. They were not to know, however, that the weekends were the busiest time at the centre, and that I would be involved helping Adrian when I wasn't at work at the hospital.

I also found the work rather slow and uninspiring. The booking days, in which we advised, examined, scanned and took bloods for ladies in early pregnancy, were very busy, and there was an unwritten code to perform these tasks as quickly as humanly possible. By lunchtime, there was usually a "competition" to see how many ladies we had managed to book that morning. Approving grunts or disdainful looks accompanied your morning's report.

The afternoons were usually midwives' clinics, and this gave a certain autonomy of practice which I really enjoyed. We only needed to contact the doctors if we discovered a problem which was outside of our remit. We could take all the blood samples, and assess the ladies, referring them for scans if necessary, and perform and interpret fetal monitoring, where this was required. But I missed the excitement of the Delivery Suite and the challenges of the postnatal ward with its occupants' wobbly hormones, and babies who needed special understanding.

The weeks rolled busily by, and I tried to combine my new job with helping Adrian at the centre. It was soon July, and the time had come for Janine and Mark's wedding. Adrian and I had planned to attend the wedding in Burnham, go to the reception, and then drive up to Adrian's parents' house in Birmingham for the remainder of the weekend.

The wedding was delightful; Janine and Mark were obviously very happy together, and we wished them all the love in the world as they departed for their honeymoon. We were still reliving our own wedding as we drove up to Birmingham. On the way, I started to feel unwell. I felt utterly drained of all energy, and my throat was sore. I dismissed it as plain tiredness, and hoped that a good night's sleep would rectify the problem.

The next day, however, I still felt rough. I didn't want to cause a fuss, so Adrian and I continued with our schedule of meeting up with Adrian's family and friends, which was great.

"Are you sure you're alright, Hil? You're looking very peaky," Adrian asked as we began the drive home.

"I feel shattered; I don't know what's the matter with me. Can't take the pace, I reckon. Don't worry, Adrain, I'm sure I'll be okay."

The next morning, I felt worse, and had developed a very itchy rash which seemed to come and go of its own accord. At times, it was like having chicken pox all over again, and the spots reared their ugly heads in the most sensitive of places. Adrian saw the rash and said that he would contact the doctor. He also rang my work and explained the situation. I felt the old guilt crashing down on me once again. I hated being off work. I was paid to do a job and I felt that I should be there, and not lying prostrate in a soaking nightdress with a rash which had a mind of its own.

The doctor visited us in the afternoon, and having examined my throat, which was extremely sore by this stage, he prescribed a course of steroids. He seemed quite impressed with the rash. "I think you have glandular fever. Did you know that only 6 per cent of sufferers end up with a rash like this?"

I wondered if this was supposed to make me feel better. He pulled a needle and syringe out of his bag, and took some bloods to confirm the diagnosis. Glandular fever, eh? I tried not to notice the knowing wink he aimed in Adrian's direction. Yes, of course I knew that it was also called "the kissing disease". Was nothing sacred?

Dr Mayberry said that he would be in again tomorrow to see how things were progressing, and I was left with my mind reeling. Glandular fever could take weeks to recover from, and I really didn't have that sort of time. I must get back to my new job, to show them that I was dedicated to my profession. The only problem was that I could hardly stand up, let alone seriously consider returning to work.

The days passed slowly, and most were spent staring at a dappled ceiling as the summer sunshine danced its way across the sky. Outside, I could hear Adrian encouraging and shepherding dozens of children as they spent their holidays with us. A fat lot of good I was to him like this, I thought.

Each week, Dr Mayberry handed me a medical certificate which explained that I was unfit for work for the following week. By the end of the seventh one, I was determined to return to work, even if it was just to show that I still wanted my job. I was getting desperate to return to the work which I loved.

"Are you sure you feel ready to return to work, Hilary?" Dr Mayberry looked searchingly over the rim of his spectacles.

"I *must* get back to work. I'd only worked there for four weeks before all this happened. They must be wondering why on earth they gave me the job in the first place."

"I do understand, Hilary, but there is no point returning before you are strong enough, is there?"

"I'm sure I'll be alright, thank you."

With that, he handed me the certificate which stated that I would be fit to return to work the following Monday. We drove to the hospital and I handed the certificate to the senior midwife who was on duty. "We were beginning to think we'd lost you," she said with a wry smile.

"I know, and I'm so sorry. I'll be back again on Monday, fighting fit."

"Let's hope so," she said as she walked away.

Chapter Eighteen

I returned to work on Monday but the following few days were a nightmare. I began to wonder if I would ever begin to feel better. Some of my colleagues were kind and suggested that I should lie down on an examination couch during our lunch breaks, to see if this would improve the situation. I just felt thoroughly embarrassed. After all, nurses, doctors and midwives aren't supposed to have health problems, are they? There is this unwritten law which states that they are supposed to keep going whilst others are ill around them. I felt a complete failure.

I did my best to persevere, but sometimes things all became too much. In spite of the fact that I had reduced my hours to 30 per week, I was repeatedly left as the last member of staff on duty in the clinic whilst the others disappeared off home. Their logic must have been that they were working full time and so deserved to leave early.

It was such a struggle to keep going that I began to feel thoroughly resentful. On one shift, I was told to work in the fertility clinic – a job about which I knew very little. It actually meant that I was a glorified hand-maiden for the doctor, and simply escorted women through to the cubicles and preserved their dignity whilst the doctor took various samples, and examined them under the microscope.

I tried to be positive and reassuring to the women as they waited for the results of various tests, but I didn't really know much more than the rudiments, and was unable to answer questions about various obscure hormone levels, etc. I felt ashamed and embarrassed, and a total disappointment to the women who were looking so earnestly to me for advice and support.

It was a very long and protracted clinic, and it was about 5:30 by the time we had seen the final patient. The antenatal clinic had long since been deserted, and I felt really frustrated by the old ghost of being taken for granted, once again. I drove home, and Adrian was looking worried. "Where have you been, Hil? You should have been home over an hour ago; I was beginning to get worried!"

I explained what had happened, and apologised for not being up to cooking dinner. Adrian's meals were supposed to be supplied by the centre, but mine were not and since our marriage, I had been cooking our evening meal so that we could eat together in peace. Adrian managed to acquire a meal for us both, and we put the money for mine in the kitty in the office. This was one of the real advantages of "living on the job".

The following week, I received a phone call from the Maternity Unit at Welwyn, asking me to apply for a sister's post which was becoming vacant there. "It's a wonderful opportunity for you, Hilary." Sister Ruby's voice was full of enthusiasm. "I am pretty sure you would get it, too. You are the sort of midwife who is born and not made, and we all know you and respect you greatly."

"Thank you so much for thinking of me. Unfortunately, I'm not very well at the moment."

"Don't worry about that. Just come over on Friday, and I'll take you through the information you will need to know, and then I'm sure you're going to be fine."

She wouldn't take no for an answer, so, in spite of the fact that I could hardly walk, Adrian drove us to the QEII hospital. It felt so strange to be back. I could feel my senses realigning to all the old procedures, sights and smells. It felt like home, and I gathered all my strength together to try to take in all the information Sister Ruby was trying to impart. It was great to see her. Throughout my training she had been my mentor and encourager. She had believed in me when I had found it very difficult to believe in myself. She was a rare and very wonderful person.

"You will apply, won't you, Hilary?"

"As long as things start to improve, I will."

We hugged each other as the lift opened its doors on the ground floor, and Adrian and I walked out into the car park clutching numerous papers with copious information concerning midwifery practice and legal issues. I felt completely drained.

"What did you think of all that, Hil?"

"Nice work if you're up to it," I replied, trying to sound humorous. We drove home, and I lay down on the settee, praying that this nightmare would come to an end SOON.

The following day I woke up feeling much worse. I began to get angry, with myself mainly, but also with God. Why had He allowed this to happen? I had been giving every ounce of my strength and determination to follow Him, and for what? In a gesture of pathetic defiance, I shook my fist at the ceiling, and kept repeating, "Why? Why?" No answer came, and I fell back on the pillows too exhausted to move any more.

I returned to work but things deteriorated further, and it all came to a head one Thursday morning when the midwives travelled by minibus to one of the outlying hospitals to perform a midwives' clinic. I had told the sister, Kate, that I was feeling particularly rough, and she had told me to work with the doctor who supported our work there.

I spent the morning checking blood pressures, and putting names on blood bottles, and filling in forms. Even this was proving too much, as I found it very difficult to concentrate. Halfway through the morning, Sister Kate came into the doctor's office. "How's it going, Hilary?"

"Well, you know," I replied.

"You look terrible. I think you'd better come through to the staff room."

I felt too weak to argue, but also rather ashamed. The doctor looked up and said, "Aren't you feeling well?" I shook my head and lamely followed Kate out of his office.

"I think you'd better lie down. Here, I've got a blanket to keep you warm – your hands are freezing!"

I lay down, and felt a complete nuisance to everyone. Time passed, and the midwives took it in turns to come in for their cups of coffee. Maria, one of the more mature midwives came over. "I've got something for you in my handbag, just a minute." She rummaged around in her bag, as women do, and brought out a newspaper cutting which was headed: "New Research: Yuppie Flu is Real". "It's about a condition called M.E. It's caused by a viral illness, and I think it's what you've got."

"Thank you so much, Maria; it's really kind of you." I clasped the cutting underneath the blankets, and tried to read it, but just could not concentrate.

194

I had heard about this "yuppie flu". It was a derogatory term for a prolonged recovery from a viral infection, and there was a lot of scepticism about its validity amongst the medical profession. Trust me to be incapacitated by something that nobody really knew very much about, and that could be maligned as an illness which was "all in the mind". I was grateful that some progress was evidently being made, and that some doctors were now beginning, at least, to believe that this illness had a genuine and very real physical cause.

Kate called Adrian and asked him to meet us at the hospital once the clinic was finished. Elizabeth drove him to Wexham Park, and then Adrian drove us home in our little Nova which we had bought to replace the Marina and Cortina.

Once we were home, we contacted the doctors' surgery and made an appointment to see Dr Haldane the following day. Things couldn't continue like this; it was ridiculous. We attended the surgery and I explained the story of the previous eight weeks. I showed him the newspaper cutting. "A friend from work was wondering whether it might be this."

Dr Haldane read the cutting and looked a little perturbed. "I don't think we should go rushing into a diagnosis without doing further tests." I didn't know whether to feel relieved or annoyed by his approach. All I wanted was to feel better so that I could be a better wife to Adrian, and get back to work.

Dr Haldane handed me a bundle of blood forms and instructed me to have the blood taken as soon as possible, and to see him again in three days' time for the results. He also handed me a medical certificate for the next two weeks. My heart sank. With each medical certificate came the feeling of failure and gloom.

The blood results didn't show anything conclusive, so it seemed that we were back to square one. Over the following week, I developed a profound weakness and pins and needles in my left leg. It became so troublesome that I could no longer walk without dragging the leg behind me. I began to think that perhaps I was going loopy after all.

I kept telling myself to buck up and get on with things, but my muscles just wouldn't be cajoled or bullied into any form of compliance. Indeed, the harder I tried to do things, the worse the symptoms became and I was trapped in a body which was no longer willing to do as it was told. Instead, it seemed to have me by the scruff of the neck, and there was no way out, other than to give in graciously to the limitations it imposed.

I found this very hard to bear, as I had always been very sporty, and I began to realise that a lot of my self-esteem arose from my professional identity. What was I, if I didn't have a job? The endless questioning and self-examination led me on a path littered with shattered dreams. All my high hopes of promotion and helping Adrian at the centre seemed to vanish before my eyes, and a terrible, creeping sense of loss seemed to relentlessly envelop my every waking moment.

At the next appointment with Dr Haldane I explained the feeling of being stuck at the bottom of a very deep, dark well, and having no means to climb out. He listened very patiently, and finally suggested that a short course of antidepressants could help things. I was angry at his suggestion. It was like adding insult to injury. I wasn't depressed; I was fighting this thing with all my strength. How dare he suggest that I needed "happy pills"?

I had always assumed that depression could be

overcome by determination. My mum's phrase, "You can, you must, and you will", seemed to haunt me now. Why wasn't I strong enough to fight this thing without having to resort to medication? I was a nurse and a midwife, and I was supposed to be strong for everyone. Why, after all the struggles of the past eight years, had I come to this now, when life should have been at its most happy and successful?

As the doctor wrote the prescription, I wanted to walk out of the surgery. "Please don't feel that you have failed in any way, Hilary," he said, as though he was reading my mind. "The Epstein Barr virus that caused your glandular fever is renowned for causing post-viral depression. I think that you are suffering from post-viral chronic fatigue. This will take some time to clear up, and you are going to have to be much more patient with yourself. I'll give you another certificate for a month, and then come and see me again, and we'll see how you're getting on."

I took the prescription reluctantly, thanked Dr Haldane for his time, and then walked slowly to the local pharmacy. I stood nervously waiting for the tablets, and felt ashamed as they were handed to me. Did the pharmacist know that I was a failure, too? I walked back to the car in tears, disappointed by my own weakness.

I sat down in the car, clutching the medical certificate and fearing the wrath of the management back at Wexham Park. I could well imagine the raised eyebrows and barbed comments with which the certificate would be received. How could I convince them that this was never my intention? I felt as though my entire credibility was on the line.

Back at home, I explained to Adrian what had

happened. "I'm so sorry about this, Adrain. I don't want to cause you all this hassle, and I'm trying to get this sorted out."

He hugged me and said, "Don't worry, Hil. Let's hope these tablets help you to feel better. And perhaps," he added, "we should try posting the medical certificates instead of having to face the powers that be?"

What an ingenious idea! I was so grateful that he understood and that he was not judging me. At the back of my mind, though, was this awful feeling of dread that he could only be expected to put up with so much, and that perhaps he would decide that our marriage had been a big mistake.

The next few days were spent feeling extremely dopey and spaced out. Whatever was in these tablets was having a profound effect on my sleep, and I felt continuously drowsy and had a mouth like the bottom of a bird cage. When I returned to the surgery for the follow-up, I was feeling pretty drugged and not much better emotionally.

"Keep going with the tablets, and I'll see you again in two weeks' time. See me sooner if you need to." The doctor handed me another medical certificate for a further month, and I despatched this by post, worried that every time the phone rang it would be someone from work telling me that I had been dismissed.

The months passed with a relentless feeling of failure and hopes dashed. I gradually came to the conclusion that I would have to let go of my dreams of becoming a midwifery sister. It was a long and painful bereavement. I had loved my work, and had found my professional calling. The Lord had blessed me so much in my job, and I had been so privileged to support couples through the dramas of pregnancy and childbirth.

For someone who had very little self-confidence, I had found a place where I could soar, and to lose it all was excruciatingly painful.

I sulked with God, and kept asking Him why He had allowed this to happen. I continued to blame myself as well, but neither avenue brought peace or understanding. With reluctance, I contacted Sister Ruby and explained the situation, and how sorry I was not to be able to apply for the sister's post at Welwyn. Gradually, I had to come to a place where I could let it go, and accept the fact that when one door closes, another opens.

Chapter Nineteen

The weeks rolled into months, and to my horror Dr Haldane increased the strength of the medication further. I felt as though I was being branded a head case, and struggled hard against the accompanying feelings of loss of autonomy. I gradually had to reach a place where it was possible to truly submit to the Lord, difficult as that was. I also had to work through the idea that He had dumped this awful illness on me, and spent many hours crying it through in prayer.

Gradually, though, the feelings of anger began to subside, and I began to accept that in all things God does work for the good of those who love Him. In spite of the continuing fatigue and exhaustion, I was beginning to see that I still mattered as a person, and that my whole being did not depend upon what I was officially able to do.

It was liberating to realise this, and I began to understand that I had spent most of my life trying to prove that I was worthy of acceptance. Now I could see that God does not look at us like that at all. In fact, what really matters to Him is that we truly trust Him, and begin to understand His unconditional love for us.

A year passed, and I was sent an officious letter from work explaining that I would no longer be entitled to sick pay. I sent a letter of resignation, and apologised wholeheartedly for the inconvenience I had caused. Another letter arrived from the Department of Social Services – I had to attend an interview to prove that I was still unfit for work. These letters threatened to disrupt my newly found but tenuous peace, and I hated the fact that I had to prove an illness which had completely disrupted my life.

The examination passed fairly well, and the doctor seemed to be very understanding, which was a considerable relief. I continued to have good and bad days, and slowly reached a point where I felt ready to return to a small part-time job, well away from the rigours of nursing.

It so happened that the centre required a new secretary, and I was delighted to be offered the job by the centre's accountant, Cyril, with whom I would work quite closely. Initially, I found that my confidence had almost completely vanished, and I had a quiet panic every time the telephone rang. But bit by bit, I began to understand all of the nuances of the various booking procedures, and developed my own letters on the word processor which improved efficiency greatly. The electric typewriter in the corner of the office was relegated to second place, and I only coaxed it into action when absolutely necessary. It seemed to have a mind of its own, and occasionally one of the keys would stick, causing all manner of irregularities. It was not uncommon for the occasional near miss in the language department to erupt from that corner of the room!

Months passed, and I gradually began to feel better. Dr Haldane agreed to let me reduce the medication, and finally to come off it altogether. I still felt weak, and tired very easily, but in my core, I felt as though my strength was returning. It was about then that I received some information from the M.E. Association, and one article in particular caught my eye. It was about M.E. and pregnancy. Apparently, there had been cases where women who were ill had become pregnant and their symptoms had improved markedly. Adrian and I had agreed before marriage that we wanted children, and we talked about this article. We spoke to Dr Haldane who suggested that it really was a risk, but if we wanted to try for a baby, then that was our decision.

During the next three months, Adrian continued to follow his call into some form of Christian ministry. He spoke with the Diocesan Director of Ordinands, who suggested that he might be best suited for a training in evangelism. Contact was made with a college in London, and an initial visit was arranged. After a nerve-racking week, Adrian discovered that he had been accepted for training in the following September. We were delighted. The centre had been a tremendous experience, but we both felt the need to move on.

A few days after this, one of Adrian's brothers came to stay with us for a short break. On his first evening, we decided to go to the local pub just around the corner from the centre, and we spent a very happy evening talking about all sorts of ridiculous things. I swapped a half pint of cider for Adrian's pint, and then had a further half pint. As we walked home, we were singing silly songs and mimicking the peacocks which lived in one of the adjacent houses. We all felt rather merry.

We walked into the flat and collapsed on the settee. Things were reeling slightly, and we couldn't seem to stop talking. And then, out of the blue Adrian's brother said, "So what does it mean, to become a Christian?" I did a double take and took a deep breath. No, that didn't seem to be working, so I simply said, "I'll make us all a cup of coffee and then we'll talk about it."

I wobbled precariously to the kitchen and prodded Adrian in the ribs. The suddenness of this request on top of a large quantity of cider made it difficult to approach this important moment without a degree of mild hysteria.

"Adrain!"

"What?"

"He wants to know how to become a Christian! Quick, hand me the coffee!"

We returned from the kitchen trying to look as calm and composed as possible, and also trying to access the brain files which would hopefully provide a clear and understandable set of answers to his questions. We had a long talk in which we described that becoming a Christian means allowing Jesus to be Lord of your life, and being willing to be led by His Holy Spirit. It is the beginning of a new life. Not that it means that you suddenly become perfect, absolutely not, but that you are willing to follow Jesus's ways, and not just do whatever you want to do.

We finished talking at about midnight, and then Adrian and I went to bed, amazed to be given this opportunity to share all that Jesus meant to us. He had loved us enough to die for us, and had always been there for us, and we trusted Him for our future.

This was just the beginning of a succession of incidents in which we could see God in action. A couple of days later, one of the visitors to the centre had problems with her car. No matter what she did, she couldn't get it to start. I suddenly had this rather strange feeling that we should lay hands on it and pray for it. Adrian and I went outside, and prayed that, in the Name of Jesus, this car would start. Jesus did say that if we prayed, believing that He would answer us, then great things would happen. It was a tremendous relief when the engine coughed, spluttered and finally agreed to return to the land of the living!

A couple of days later, we had a group of men staying at the centre, and the boiler broke down. It was the weekend and the weather was beginning to get chilly, and we were told that we were unlikely to receive a visit from an engineer until Monday. We tried flicking all the relevant switches time and time again, but nothing seemed to happen. So Adrian and I knelt by the boiler, and prayed that, in the Name of Jesus, it would work.

The boiler burst into life, and the comical reaction was that the men then complained that the water was too hot! We were experiencing, first-hand, the generosity of God. He didn't just fix things, but He fixed them abundantly.

Following this, we came across an unwanted spiritual visitor at the centre one evening. We had just returned from the Baptist church in Slough where the worship was wonderful, when I sensed a very troubling presence down the hallway into the dining room. I felt my spine go cold, and my heart started beating wildly. I could sense a malicious presence. I grabbed Adrian, and we started to pray aloud, and to praise the Name of Jesus Who brings peace and life and hope. We prayed that this presence would be returned to a place of rest in His Name.

All the while, I was terrified that something visible would appear. I am not a brave soul when it comes to this sort of thing, but I clung to the words in the Bible where Jesus gave authority to His disciples to deal with evil spirits. We carried on praying for about half an hour, and gradually felt able to walk down to the dining room, declaring Christ's victory, and proclaiming His peace.

And peace finally came. Adrian and I eventually went upstairs, exhausted and very relieved.

A couple of weeks later, Adrian had to journey into London to spend a pre-college weekend getting to know his fellow students. As the centre was due to be empty, and I didn't like staying there alone, Steve and Elizabeth had offered to let me stay in their flat for the weekend. Adrian left on the Friday evening, and I felt lonely and missed him terribly, but Steve and Elizabeth were kind and generous and we had a good giggle.

On the Sunday, I returned to the flat to find that there had been a leak in one of the pipes in our bathroom. The carpet was completely sodden, and Paul, Adrian's new assistant, had removed the carpet and hung it on the line to dry. Normally, I would have spent the next couple of hours mopping up the remaining water, but I had this incredibly insistent feeling that I just had to be at church. I grumbled with the Lord about it, and asked Him if it was absolutely necessary, but all that came back was a sense of great anticipation.

I headed off to the church, and was later than usual. Instead of sitting at the front, I found a seat opposite the side entrance door. All the way through the first half of the service, I felt an increasing anticipation that something very important was going to happen.

It didn't come as much of a surprise, therefore, when a few moments later, the door opened, and a young woman whom I had never seen walked shyly in. I knew then that this was the reason why I had to be in church. I moved over in the pew, and offered her my service book. "Hullo," I said. "It's really nice to see you."

There was an immediate connection between us,

206

and it reminded me of the time in Edinburgh when the Lord had let me to a bus stop to speak to a young woman called Sophie, who I had never met before, but who was ready to ask Jesus into her life. That had been a God-anointed appointment, and I knew that this was another one. The service continued, and I tried to steer Yvonne through the intricacies of hymns which are ancient and not so modern.

At the end of the service, we had a cup of coffee, and then I had this awful feeling that I should invite her home. Now I had to battle with this one because the flat was in rather a state owing to the burst pipe, and I was rather house-proud, and didn't want anyone to see it as it was. There was also the small issue of food. I only had enough for one person. But the feeling persisted, and I finally blurted out the offer of lunch to this poor girl. I definitely am not the most spontaneous of hostesses, but Jesus seemed to be asking me to do this.

"Thank you, I'd love to come," she said.

We walked along the lane to the centre, talking about Yvonne's work, her family and friends. I asked her what had brought her to church, and she talked about an increasing hunger for God, and how she felt that the time had come to find Him. I couldn't believe it. Here was someone else who was ready to come to faith. I wished that Adrian was there; he would have known what to do far better than me – he was the evangelist, wasn't he?

I stabbed the frozen minced beef into some sort of submission, and it eventually cooked. Surprisingly, there was plenty there for us both. Our conversation continued, and I tried very hard not to be too pushy, but it was obvious that Yvonne was ready to come to a point of committing her life to Jesus. I found one of our little leaflets which explained what becoming a

Christian really means, and how to pray, asking for God's forgiveness for things that have happened in the past, and asking Jesus to become Lord of your life. Yvonne read the leaflet carefully, and then looked up.

"I want to pray this prayer now."

"Are you sure?"

"Yes. God has been calling me for years, and now I know that I want to follow Him."

"Okay, then, Yvonne. You pray, and I will sit with you whilst you do it."

It was immensely touching as she bowed her head, and with a trembling voice read out the prayer of repentance and asked Jesus to become Lord of her life. In my own spirit, I could sense an elation which was beyond words. I knew that this was a very significant moment, and that a great victory had been won in this young woman's life on this day. I prayed for God's blessing and protection upon her, and that He would guide her by His peace. Then we went out for a walk in the nearby fields, and I could tell that she felt infused with light and hope. I was humbled to be present at this spiritual rebirth. I marvelled that the Lord should let someone like myself, who in many senses was a failure, be part of something so special. Being a midwife had been incredible, but this was even more wonderful.

Later on that afternoon, Adrian returned from London, having thoroughly enjoyed his weekend. I introduced him to Yvonne, and we spent a couple of hours chatting, and then she left for her home.

"I thought I was the evangelist," Adrian laughed as he shut the door on the outside world.

"Exactly. And where were you? At college, learning how to be an evangelist!"

The next day I continued my vigil, praying for a

baby of our own. I had spent the past four months praying, more and more desperately, asking God for this most precious gift. We went to a study day at St Andrew's Chorleywood with Colin, our vicar. Towards the end of the day, there were several "words of knowledge" about various medical problems. This was a time when members of the ministry team who were open to the Holy Spirit, received an understanding of some of the problems being experienced by members of the congregation.

There was a word of knowledge about a painful back, a painful leg, and even haemorrhoids. Following this, there was a call to come to the front if you were trying to conceive. I sat rooted to the spot, going through one of those "Oh no, it can't mean I've go to do something about this" moments.

I rose from my seat rather nervously, and passed a whole group of very wise-looking and learned men and women. "I'm not going up for the haemorrhoids," I said rather stupidly as I walked past. Once there, I waited patiently for one of the women who were praying for others, to become available. I don't know why it is, but it's always at these most sacred moments that I feel ever so slightly unreal. I'm definitely not a true Anglican, because I always want to laugh at moments such as these.

"What is it you are wanting prayer for?" the woman asked.

I bit my lower lip hard and took a deep breath. "I dearly want to have a baby, please." The "please" was a bit unnecessary because she was not about to hand me a baby in a bundle, was she? She and her friend prayed that I would go forth and multiply, and I felt rather silly. I only wanted one baby after all.

Two days later, I was beginning to feel rather sick, and my period was late. I sidled into the local pharmacy and, with shaking hands, bought a home pregnancy kit. The next morning, Adrian and I were sitting in bed, whilst the results of the test became evident. A blue line slowly appeared, and in those few minutes, I knew that our lives would be changed forever. I kept hiding under the covers and popping up again saying, "Oh my God! Oh my God!" We were both elated and terrified at the same time.

The first few weeks after that were spent with an insatiable hunger for pickled onion-flavoured corn puffs. I felt a bit obvious going into the local supermarket and filling the basket with only these. I hoped that the lady at the checkout would be of an understanding disposition. She took it with great equanimity, and simply kept repeating, "Thank you very much, thank you. Thank you very much, thank you." She must have said that hundreds of times a day, and I wondered where her thoughts were whilst she repeated her mantra.

Back at the centre, life was getting even more interesting. We had to employ a new cook, and eventually an applicant arrived, who on paper seemed to be well qualified. After a few weeks, however, our concerns for her were increasing on an exponential scale.

Sharon was very fond of keeping fit – so fond, that she had even gone to the extremes of taking medication from a health shop which was supposed to help her lose fat and build up her muscles. She had been gradually becoming a little edgy and vague, and her cooking had slowly become rather wayward.

One Friday evening, a group of young people arrived for the weekend and Sharon presented them with fish, chips and soggy cauliflower. It just seemed a little odd. Over the weekend, however, things went from being a little odd to verging on the psychotic.

Adrian and I had just sat down in our living room on the Sunday evening when the group had gone home, when there was a knock at our door. Sharon entered the flat, wringing her hands, and staring about her in wide-eyed fear. "I know it's in there," she kept saying.

"What's in where, Sharon?" I tried to sound reassuring.

"It's a dark figure. It's in my flat. I know it's in there."

Now, I don't know about you, but when someone says something like that, I want to run a mile.

"There's nothing sinister in your flat, Sharon." I was glad that Adrian was keeping a grip on the situation.

She began to pace up and down our living room, unable to relax or to sit down. She had a fixed, terrified expression in her eyes. Whatever she had seen, or thought she had seen, it had really frightened her. The really scary thing was that we just were not getting through to her at all, and she was locked into this terrible fear.

The hours passed, and Adrian offered to go down to Sharon's flat whilst I stayed with her in our own. He arrived back a few minutes later, his face a combination of relief and annoyance.

"Is everything alright?" I asked.

Adrian grimaced, and then spoke directly to Sharon. "I think that it hasn't helped that you've been reading all those books on the occult, has it, Sharon?"

"I know it's in there," she replied.

I took Adrian out to our kitchen. "I think that she is having an acute psychiatric episode, and we really need to contact her doctor."

"Okay." We returned to the living room, and tried to persuade Sharon that this would be the most helpful way forward, but she only became more agitated.

"You can't call my doctor. I won't let you!" She continued to pace more fervently, and I had this awful feeling that everything was spiralling out of control.

"Would you like us to take you back to your flat, and we can pray for God's blessing upon you and your flat?" I was running out of ideas. Sharon looked terrified, but she finally agreed to let us pray for her there. When we entered the room, it was littered with books on the occult, ranging from witchcraft to devil worship. I shuddered inwardly. This really went against the grain.

We began to pray for God's blessing and peace upon Sharon and her home, and we proclaimed Christ's light and life to overcome all darkness and fear. She gradually relaxed, and said that she would be alright for the rest of the night. We left her sitting on the end of her bed, tidying away her books.

We went to bed, and about half an hour later, were very upset to hear the sound of the centre's minibus being driven away at high speed. We spent the next few hours waiting up like anxious parents for an errant teenager to return home. Eventually, we went to sleep. The next morning, we were making breakfast when she drove back. We rushed outside to see her.

"Where have you been? We've been really worried about you!"

"I went to an all-night rave in London," she stated, as though that was the most natural thing in the world.

"Are you alright now?" I tried to sound understanding, and not too angry.

"Why shouldn't I be?" she glowered, and then swept past me into her flat, and shut the door.

A few months later, we had a group of young teenagers staying with us, courtesy of one of the Oxford colleges. The young people were full of high spirits, and were quite a difficult group to control. The students who were in charge were doing their best, and tried to ensure that nobody came to any harm. Adrian was on hand to help supervise and to give helpful ideas to maintain the group's cohesiveness.

We finally made it to the penultimate day, the Friday, which just happened to be the Thirteenth. The students had had the bright idea of renting the film of the same name, after which, they completely lost control of their charges.

A fight broke out in the living room. One of the youngsters smashed a wooden stool and started running around the centre threatening to kill anyone who got in his way. The girls were screaming hysterically because one of them was sure that she'd seen a face outside the window, looking in. Another young lad managed to grab a large kitchen knife, and began to threaten someone he'd spent the entire week sparring against. It was only the Grace of God, and the quick-wittedness of the helpers which prevented a stabbing.

Everyone was shaken. Adrian and I had been sitting upstairs in our living room when we heard the commotion. We ran downstairs, and Adrian immediately took charge of the youngsters, while I took the helpers up to our flat so that they could recover.

We finally managed to calm everyone down, but had to resort to driving the group around the entire grounds in the minibus before they could be convinced that there wasn't anyone lurking in the undergrowth. And people say that television doesn't affect kids.

By the time they left the following day, it was difficult to decide who was the most exhausted. It had been a potentially very dangerous situation, and it confirmed our feelings that we were nearing the end of our ability to enjoy such happenings in the middle of the night. This, together with the fact that guests to the main house often discovered our own private bathroom and would happily wander into our flat to use it, made us feel that the time to move on couldn't come soon enough.

Chapter Twenty

Before the move could happen, however, there were just a few loose ends to tie up, not least the matter of giving birth for the first time. Now, it's all very well knowing the theory, but it's quite another matter when it comes to putting that theory into practice.

Throughout the months, the baby had been quietly growing, and I had felt a resurgence in my own strength. Once the morning sickness began to abate, and we had passed the crucial thirteen-week barrier, I began to feel more alive than ever before. The last vestiges of M.E. vanished, and with the coming of the spring, I felt like a new woman. I felt more alive, as though I could finally be kind to myself for the sake of the baby. I enjoyed all the trappings of pregnancy, even down to the tent-like dungarees. Most of all, though, I loved feeling the baby move inside me.

When this first happened, I was in a meeting with Cyril, the accountant, and Adrian, discussing cash flow and booking numbers for the following month. We were approaching various companies asking for sponsorship to replace the aging minibus, when I felt the first kick. I stopped in mid-sentence and held my breath. Adrian and Cyril did the same. "Are you alright, Hil?"

"I've just felt the baby move! Oh, I can't believe it! It gave me such a kick!"

The meeting lost some of its momentum at this stage, but we did our best to return to the topic in question. Once Cyril had gone, we rushed upstairs to see if we could feel the baby kicking any more.

Everything progressed normally for the next few months until about six months into the pregnancy when my blood pressure began to rise. I was advised to rest and to take it easy. I did try, but it was difficult. I was feeling better than ever, the days were becoming warm and sunny, and my friends at church were full of womanly understanding. It felt great to be alive, and at the centre of this most miraculous act of creation.

Each trip to the antenatal clinic, however, revealed an increasing blood pressure, and I began to worry that something would be wrong with the baby.

"Don't worry about it, Hilary," the doctor had said. "We'll send out the community midwife to check you twice a week, and then see how things go. Remember to rest."

But the blood pressure just wouldn't settle, so I was admitted to hospital for rest for five days, and spent most of that time sitting like a ripening lemon on a hospital bed. At the back of my mind, though, was this awful feeling that perhaps there was something wrong. My mind kept returning to my last delivery, and I was haunted by the images of that little baby's face. I continued to pray that the Lord would look after my little child who was precious beyond words.

The bed rest in hospital did the trick and I was allowed home for good behaviour, where I plodded around anxiously, trying to be all relaxed but not succeeding very well.

One day, I went out to Eton Wick to buy something from the pharmacy there. As I got out of the car, a yellow Rolls Royce parked in front of me. I knew that Ernie Wise drove one of these, and that he lived nearby, so I peered at the car's occupant as he climbed out. Sure enough, it was him. This threw me into a complete panic. I had loved all of his programmes since I was very young, and I couldn't believe that he was here, in the flesh.

I suddenly decided that I would go into another shop because I wasn't sure that I could be trusted to hold down an intelligent conversation with a television icon at that particular moment. I felt disappointed with myself when the yellow Rolls Royce drove away, and I had failed to ask for his autograph. A missed opportunity.

The last few weeks of the pregnancy dragged on. The summer was reaching its peak, and the grass on the lawns had become white with heat and the lack of rain. I began swelling up like a proverbial balloon, and could be found on certain occasions, sitting with my feet in a bucket of cold water, a cool flannel draped over the bump, which was now an impressive size.

We were hosting the annual Dorney Fête in the grounds of the centre, and Adrian had spent a lot of time coordinating events for the big day. The villagers had very kindly decided to use this opportunity to officially thank Adrian for all his hard work over the past six years, and to wish us well when we moved away in about four weeks' time.

Just before everyone arrived, I removed the cold flannels, dressed, and tried very hard not to waddle too much as I wandered around the various stalls within the grounds. Everyone had put so much effort into their creations, and it was great to see so much cooperation and good will. There was the welly-throwing competition in one corner of the lawn, and a cake and jam stall directly opposite to that. Children were waiting patiently for donkey rides towards the back of the house, and the air was filled with laughter and the smell of sun-baked earth. I was going to miss living here.

As I walked slowly around the house, smiling and waving to friends and acquaintances, I thought back to the evenings we had spent in these grounds, hosting the children's holidays and playing rounders with sponges so that everyone got wet. I remembered the prayer meetings and youth groups which we had led in the house itself, and of course, all the hard-working people to whom the centre owed its very existence.

As the summer sunshine bathed us all in its benevolent warmth, I felt full of praise to God. It had been an incredible privilege to live in this place, rubbing shoulders with the highly educated and successful residents who lived in this locality, and yet meeting people who were extremely needy and who had used this as a place of refuge and recreation.

Yet the Lord seemed to be moving us on, and all the wheels were in motion for this to happen in the third week in August. As Adrian and I cut our farewell cake and sipped champagne, it was a bittersweet moment.

But time was marching on, and I was getting progressively more desperate to deliver this little child who seemed to have taken a liking to kicking my liver with particular consistency. I was beginning to think that there just wasn't any room left for further growth, and had resorted to sitting in a most ungainly fashion when there wasn't anyone watching.

Weekly antenatal visits continued, and the baby's due date, the 27th of July, came and went most uneventfully. Three days later, I rolled up to the hospital, look-ing and feeling rather desperate. I had visions of the baby still not having been born by the time we were due to move in three weeks' time.

"Your blood pressure is up again, Hilary. I really think that we should induce your labour and get this baby delivered."

"Okay," I said, rather glibly. "When do you want to do it?"

"Tomorrow."

"Tomorrow?"

"No time to lose. Go home, get your bag and come back to the antenatal ward at five o'clock. We'll begin the induction with the prostaglandin gel tonight."

I nodded dumbly. My baby could be born by this time tomorrow! Adrian drove us home, and I felt rather flustered. "Don't worry, Hil. I'm sure everything will be alright."

At the back of my mind, however, was this nagging feeling that something was bound to go wrong. It almost seems to be an unwritten law that whenever doc-tors, midwives or nurses are admitted to hospital for something, there are usually some complications. I pushed the thought firmly away, along with the images of the dead baby from my last delivery at Welwyn. We got in the car, and drove back to the hospital.

We were shown to a side room and duly admitted, and I sat on the bed, having progressed from the ripen-ing lemon stage to being more of a grapefruit, waiting for the hours to pass before the prostaglandin gel would be inserted. I felt very nervous. It wasn't just that I was terrified of the prospect of pain, but also because after all these months of waiting to see my baby, the time had finally come.

Would I be able to love him or her? Supposing I turned out to be a terrible mother who did everything wrongly? The full realisation of the fact that years of work, nurture, patience and total commitment lay ahead suddenly seemed to hit me like a ton of bricks. I felt weepy and afraid. I tried to pray, but my mind was too busy to find a place of peace. I just hoped that the Lord knew what He was doing by letting me become a mother, and that He wouldn't desert me now.

I sat and wrote the baby a letter. In it I tried to convey the love that I felt for him or her, and how much I wanted to meet them, and yet how scared I felt at the same time. I had just finished writing when the doctor came in with the prostaglandin gel. "This might make you feel a little uncomfortable overnight, but I'm sure you know that already."

I nodded, trying to look relaxed, but have never mastered the art of relaxation whilst a complete stranger has his hand in one's most intimate of places.

"Thank you very much," I said as I heaved up the enormous pants. "I'm sure I'll be fine."

Little did I know, but the night which followed was ruined by intense, period-like pains which had me doubled over. By seven o'clock I was convinced that I must have started labour, but the examination revealed only a little progress. It seemed as though this could be a very long day.

At nine o'clock Adrian and I walked round to the labour ward, and we set out all our bits and pieces, music cassettes, books, flannels – everything necessary to prepare for a long haul. The doctor came in and ruptured the membranes, and what seemed like gallons of warm liquid went straight up my back and all over the floor. "You've had a lot of fluid in there," he remarked, quite unnecessarily, I thought.

The midwife, Eileen, helped to mop me up, and then I got off the bed in readiness for a day spent walking up and down to accelerate the labour. I made it to the window and then was doubled up in pain. The contractions, which usually begin slowly and gradually intensify, went straight in at nine point zero on the Richter scale. I staggered back to the bed, not quite knowing what to do. This wasn't how it usually happened to other women. I was supposed to be breathing gently and getting on with a crossword, not buckling on my knees with the first contraction.

I climbed onto the bed, moaning pathetically. I tried to remember the breathing techniques: in … two … three … four … , out … two … three … four … Adrian put on the cassette, and some jolly worship music filled the room. The contraction gradually eased and I relaxed, thinking that I'd have at least five minutes before the next one came crashing on the scene.

A minute later, however, and there was a repeat performance. Eileen came into the room. "How's it going?"

"I need an epidural," I said. Manners seemed to be on the slide.

Eileen smiled and strapped me up to the fetal monitor. "Let's just see how the baby is doing, shall we?" I grinned through gritted teeth. The monitor showed that the baby's heart rate was fine, and also that my contractions were huge and very frequent. It wasn't my imagination. My labour had gone from zero to fully established in the space of five minutes. From that time on, I was playing catch-up.

The anaesthetist arrived to administer the

epidural, but I was busily trying to eat a pillow at the time, whilst perching precariously on the delivery bed. "Would you like an epidural, Mrs Cotterill?"

"I'm terribly sorry," I mumbled in a quite incoherent fashion, "but I don't think I'm going to be able to stay still for long enough for you to complete the procedure." I had seen many women in this situation before. It is imperative that the patient is still whilst the needle is inserted into the spine in order to safely administer the epidural. I knew that there was no way I could comply for long enough for this to happen. The contractions were barely giving me 45 seconds rest between them.

"Perhaps we should try some pethidine, then?"

I tried to smile in gratitude, but was finding that the smiling muscles had been totally usurped by the grimacing ones. I really didn't want to have an injection. I felt that I should be as alert as possible during the labour, but the pain was just too horrendous. I nodded dumbly and a couple of minutes later Eileen returned with a syringeful of what I hoped would be my saving grace.

Whilst it took effect, she offered me some Entonox. I took two or three puffs and promptly threw up. "I'm so sorry," I said as the bran flakes made intricate patterns over the highly polished floor. It was true to say that things were not going strictly according to plan.

A few minutes later and the pethidine began to kick in. I can't say that it helped much with the pain, because with every contraction I felt as though my entire body was completely out of my control, but it did have the rather fascinating effect of turning the single clock at the end of the bed into six which danced around quite of their own accord.

Adrian was doing a wonderfully supportive job, mopping my brow and muttering words of encouragement. All was going well until the cassette tape came to an end, and he asked me if I would like him to put on the other side, right in the middle of a huge contraction.

"NO!" I growled, and thought I was quite controlled in not adding anything else besides.

"Okay," he said, and I could feel him exchange glances with Eileen.

I'd exchanged glances with dozens of fathers in exactly the same situation. I remember one man whose wife had attended antenatal classes with a well-known organisation. She had been in the throes of labour when he said, "Now, Helen, remember to open up like a flower, and blow the candles out with your breathing."

I thought at the time that she must have been a very understanding woman. Anything further from flowers and candles was hard to imagine in a situation like this. I carried on gasping and groaning and wondering how long this ordeal could possibly last. The labour had galloped off without me, and I was left wallowing in its wake and completely at its mercy.

Two more hours passed, and I was told that I was now ready to start pushing. The labour had been so fast and furious that things had progressed at three times the normal rate. I still felt groggy from the injection, but sat up and began pushing.

"Keep going, Hilary," said Eileen. "You need to push much harder and longer if you're going to get this baby out."

That's all very well for you to say, I thought, *but it's not your body being split apart here, is it?* I said nothing but continued to grimace most impressively, I thought, and pushed as hard as the pethidine would allow.

Two hours followed in which I pushed until I could manage no more. Still the baby would not make an appearance. "I just can't do this," I said. "I think I need some help."

One of the registrars was called. Why do they always have such large hands? After a quick examination he said, "The baby's head is just there, Hilary; you can push it out." But the contractions had decided to call it a day. They had done their bit, for goodness' sake, and had all but gone on strike. A drug was added to the intravenous drip, and a few minutes later we were back in business.

Whoever said that the pushing part of labour is the best bit must be a masochist. I felt sure that my entire nether regions were about to spill out onto the bed. "Keep going, Hilary, you're nearly there! You'll be so pleased when you've done this yourself!"

I glowered at Eileen and came to the conclusion that we really couldn't spend much more of the day like this. I pushed with all of my strength, and just as I felt that this baby would never be born, his little head appeared, quickly followed by his shoulders and body.

There was a tiny splutter and I looked down to see a very disgruntled, squashed and compact little human being lying on the bed in front of me. I couldn't believe it – he was finally here. And he was Peter.

Debbie, the second midwife, took him over to the trolley to give him some oxygen. "Don't worry, Hilary, it's probably the pethidine which is stopping him from breathing properly." But I was worried. I could see by the expression on her face that things were not as well as they might be.

"I'll just get the paediatrician to have a look at him." I really began to worry when she bundled my little son in his blankets and rushed him out of the room, which was now strangely quiet. Adrian and I looked at each other. We said nothing, but felt an awful dread creep over us. There couldn't be anything wrong with our little boy, could there?

We forced the thought to the back of our minds, and tried to be upbeat about everything when the auxiliary nurse came in to help me wash. We drank a cup of tea and ate some toast and waited patiently to be told when we could see Peter.

"He's gone to Special Care, Hilary," the sister said. "You can go and visit him in a few minutes."

We trundled up there and cuddled Peter, who seemed to be quite comfortable. "He's having a little difficulty with his breathing, so we're putting him in some head box oxygen for the moment. The consultant is going to have a look at him in a little while. You go back to the ward and have a rest. We'll let you know as soon as there is any news."

We gratefully returned to the ward, and Adrian returned home for a change of shirt. I sank back into the pillows, but just as I did so, the paediatric consultant appeared.

"I'm very sorry to have to tell you, Hilary, but we think that there is something seriously wrong with your son."

I was thunderstruck. "What do you mean? What is the matter with him?"

"We think that he has a tracheo-oesophageal fistula – where the oesophagus is blind-ending and any milk which he would swallow would end up in his lungs. I'm afraid that he may well need surgery, and we are going to have to transfer him to Great Ormond Street Hospital as a matter of urgency."

I didn't know what to say. What could I say? My baby, for whom I had prayed and yearned, could die. It was too terrible for words. A shutter went down in my mind. "Okay," I said, "I'll telephone my husband and let him know."

One of the midwives wheeled me to a telephone, and the phone was answered by Adrian's assistant, Paul. "Hi, Hilary! Congratulations! Adrian's just told me the fantastic news!" He was so full of enthusiasm and I bit my lip hard so that I didn't start blubbering. Adrian had to be able to hear what I had to say. As I waited for him to come to the phone, I tried to think of a way of breaking the news which wouldn't panic him.

"Hiya, Hil! Is everything alright?"

"You need to come back, Adrain. The doctors think there is something wrong with Peter. They've advised us to have him baptised. Can you get in touch with Colin? I know it's his day off, but he really needs to be here." The lip-biting resumed as Adrian's shocked voice came down the phone.

"Right ... okay ... right. What's the matter with Peter?"

"I'll explain when you get here," I squeaked.

"Okay, I'm on my way. Don't worry, Hil. I'm sure everything is going to be alright."

I put the phone down and dissolved into tears. Sally, the midwife, put her arms around my shoulders. "I'm sorry," I said. "It's just that it's been a terrible day."

I was taken back to Special Care and allowed to cuddle Peter. He seemed such a robust little baby, chunky and well nourished. His little face was looking less squashed and I covered it with kisses. "Please don't leave me," I whispered as I held him close to my heart.

A little while later, Adrian and Colin arrived and they set everything up in readiness for Peter's baptism. To our astonishment and delight, five members of the medical and nursing team said that they wanted to take part in the service, and they actively supported us all in prayer.

Even as I held Peter in my arms, and we all prayed, there was a tremendous sense of the presence of the Lord. A feeling of complete peace came in the place of the raw fear which had been rampaging through my heart. A quietness came over us all, and a peace beyond description filled the room. I knew that, whether Peter was allowed to live or whether Jesus would take him home, that he would be alright, and that he would be safe. In that moment, I knew that I had to surrender Peter to Him, trusting that he would do what was right for our little child.

A couple of hours later, the ambulance arrived to transfer Peter to Great Ormond Street Hospital. We were not allowed to go with him because they did not have any facilities for newly delivered mothers available at that time. Adrian and I were left to pace the room at Wexham Park until the next morning when we would drive down to be with him.

That night, Adrian was allowed to sleep in the room with me, and the staff made up a bed for him on the floor. We were shell-shocked and exhausted. This time when we should have been bonding with our little son was being stolen from us. I so longed to hold him and feed him, but my arms were empty and my heart was breaking.

We drove into London through the heat of early August. We had to park a small distance from the hospital, and as I struggled up the steps to the main entrance someone held open a door for us and said, "Oh, when is your baby due?"

"My baby is in the hospital," I answered curtly.

We walked on past the kiosks and the tiled floors and walls, and eventually found the directions to the ward. As we entered, I tried to keep my emotions under control. The consultant had told us that Peter would be having tests first thing in the morning, and that we would have to wait for the results. Would he need surgery? Was he going to live or die?

As we approached his little cot, I felt myself slip into midwife mode. The doctor was having difficulty inserting an intravenous cannula into Peter's foot. I offered to hold the foot, and spoke to Peter as I would have spoken to someone else's child. This way, I would not have to feel his pain. I knew that I should be feeling differently, but a shutter had come down in my mind, and instead of feeling closeness to this little child, I felt a reserve, a holding back.

The consultant entered the room. "It's good news, Mrs Cotterill. We've completed the tests on Peter and we've found that he has no fistula."

"Can we take him home, please?"

"I'm afraid that he does have a chest infection, probably brought about by the long second stage of labour. He will need intravenous antibiotics for four more days, so we cannot let you drive him home. You will have to wait for him to be transferred via ambulance."

"I am a midwife. I'm sure that I could take care of him in the car," I protested.

"I'm afraid that it goes against hospital policy. You will have to wait for an ambulance." With that, he turned and walked out of the room.

We spent several hours with Peter and then, on the

understanding that he would be transferred back to Wexham Park shortly, we returned to the hospital to await his arrival.

We waited, and the afternoon wore on, but still no sign of Peter. Every couple of hours I walked round to Special Care to ask them to check on his progress, but the answer which kept coming back was that we had to wait, and that an ambulance would come when one was available.

I hardly slept that night. I wanted my baby, but where was he? The journey to Special Care became a regular event, with reassurances that Peter would soon be with us, but still there was no sign of him. By the time a second night had passed, I was getting truly desperate. Adrian and I could do nothing. If we drove back to London, we would possibly miss Peter coming in the other direction. We felt powerless. Would he know how much we were longing to be with him, how much we loved him? I tried not to cry, but as I sat on the edge of my bed, surrounded by flowers, chocolates and teddies, I felt like a fraud. Where was the guest of honour?

Eventually, on the third day, we received news that Peter had arrived back. As I approached his cot, I felt nervous, frightened. Would he know how much I felt that I had let him down? As I looked at him, I was shocked to see how much he had changed. If he had been with me all the time, I would barely have noticed the smoothing of the wrinkles, the changing of the shape of his head, or the development of the jaundice which is so common in the newborn. He looked so different.

"Can I hold him?" I asked the Special Care sister.

"Of course you can; just be careful of the cannula in his foot."

I picked Peter up so carefully, like a person who

has never held a baby before. This was my baby, my very own. He wriggled slightly, stretched, and grimaced. "I think he may be getting hungry," Sister said.

And now the moment of truth came. After all the years spent helping mothers to feed their babies, now it was my turn, and it wasn't as easy as it looked. I was all fingers and thumbs, but Peter seemed to know what to do. I'd been worried that he wouldn't take to breast-feeding after being fed from a bottle by the nurses in London, but everything seemed to be okay. The only problem was that he was used to having his tummy filled from a bottle, and my body needed time to catch up with sufficient milk production. Consequently I soon became very sore.

Peter stayed in Special Care for that night, and the staff came to wake me when he needed a feed. I couldn't believe how poleaxed I felt by the time morning arrived. Getting up every two hours throughout the night would take some getting used to. The following night, Peter was allowed to stay in the room with me. I had managed to get to sleep, when suddenly, the apnoea alarm sounded from his little cot.

This was an alarm which detected lack of respiratory effort from a baby. If the baby failed to take a breath for fifteen seconds, then the alarm sounded. I nearly fell out of bed. I rushed to his cot, and with my hands shaking, I lifted him out. One of the midwives came rushing into my room. "Is everything alright in here?"

"The alarm went off," I said, rather unnecessarily.
"Is he alright?"

"I think so," I said, as I stroked his little face. He seemed to be breathing well, and his colour seemed satisfactory, as far as I could tell in the dimmed lights.

"Oh, it was probably just the monitor. He seems fine. Don't worry, just go back to sleep." Easier said than done. I placed Peter gently back in the cot, and spent the rest of the night with my eyes glued to him, feeding him every two hours.

By morning, I was exhausted, but we had visitors. Irene and Bob arrived, laden with beautiful gifts. I tried to be alert, enthusiastic and intelligible but failed somewhat. I could feel great waves of emotion crashing down upon me. I just wanted someone to come and tell me that everything really was alright, and that we weren't going to lose Peter, because, in spite of the peace which had surrounded us at his baptism, I still worried incessantly that something awful was going to happen to him.

As Irene left, I began to cry.

"You've got the blues, that's all," said Winifred as she performed our postnatal checks. "He's a lovely baby. You'll be okay." But it seemed that the more people told me that we would be fine, the more anxious and frightened I became. Perhaps things would improve when we got home?

Chapter Twenty-One

We were eventually allowed home when Peter's course of antibiotics came to an end. We carried him rather tentatively to the car, and winced and held our breaths as we drove over the smallest of bumps on the road. We were parents now, and we had responsibilities.

Dr Haldane had warned me not to breastfeed the baby during the night because he said that I should try to get as much sleep as possible, and let Adrian share the overnight feeds. But sleeping seemed to be the last thing on the agenda. Since the apnoea alarm incident, I found it impossible to rest properly, and I shot out of bed at the slightest snuffle from the little moses basket at the side of the bed. Adrian must have thought that he was now married to the female version of Zebedee.

Not only were we readjusting to this new little person, who was very vocal if things did not go strictly according to his wishes, but we were also in the process of preparing to move to the college in London. We had only two and a half weeks from the time Peter and I were discharged, before the removals van would draw up outside the flat and expect to transport all our worldly belongings through the thronging streets and across the Thames to the south-east of the big city.

To the outsider, I suppose that one could say that

this was a very exciting time. We were on the crest of a wave. Adrian was following his call into Christian ministry, and I had fulfilled my dreams to become a mother. But I felt dreadful. All of the anticipated feelings of fulfilment and success seemed to elude me. My confidence was completely shattered. I found it difficult to make any decisions without asking Adrian first, and I was so tired all the time, yet could not rest.

After one week of motherhood, disturbed nights, and various painful bits of anatomy, all I wanted was a day off. But I knew that this was impossible. I felt that there was nobody who could look after Peter properly. Supposing something happened to him, and I wasn't there to help him? I would never forgive myself. So I became emotionally chained to this little child who worried me more than words could say, and whom I loved but felt compelled to stay close to, even when it wasn't necessary.

The morning of the move dawned sunny and hot. As our furniture was prised and coaxed down the stairs at the back of the house, I sat feeding Peter, sitting on an upturned dustbin. So this was our big day, the start of the next chapter of our adventure. I felt exhausted.

We said our goodbyes to Paul and the rest of the staff, and then followed the lorry out of the drive, and headed off to our new home. For some reason, I felt sadness more than excitement. I hoped and prayed that this would be the beginning of something wonderful for us all, but there was something at the back of my mind which was advising caution. Be careful; don't rush in with both feet.

But we *were* rushing in. There was no other way to follow this calling unless we did it wholeheartedly, and that was the way in which we had both approached

234

everything in our marriage. As we pulled up alongside our new home, which looked very like a piece from a Monopoly set, there was a strange feeling of becoming linked to an organisation which was bigger than us, dominant, almost omnipotent. Even as we walked into the house I felt something in my stomach resist. I'm not going to be the conformist wife here. They cannot dictate what Adrian and I do all the time.

We attended a service which was intended to welcome all the new students, and I cuddled Peter closely throughout. On the surface, everyone seemed to be very pleasant, but I was nagged by this feeling of fear. I kept putting it down to the fact that I was overtired. I had just had a baby. I hadn't slept properly for over three weeks. We had just moved house. How many more excuses did I need?

Adrian's course began, and within a few weeks, he was seconded to a six-week placement in Sheffield. I couldn't believe it. We approached the powers that be and asked for a local placement so that we could support each other as we adjusted to parenthood, but the request was promptly met with the words, "If you cannot cope, then perhaps you are not suitable for this training" – how reminiscent of the nursing powers.

Of course we had no choice. We had given up everything to follow this course. Adrian had even raised all the funding for his course from the churches near Dorney where many people had recognised his gifts in evangelism and youth work. We felt that we owed it to all these people to continue, and to try our best to make this work.

Adrian had to go to Sheffield, and I was left wondering how I was supposed to cope with a baby who would not stop crying. Whatever I did, Peter cried. If I cuddled him, he cried. If I fed him, he cried. If I took him out for a walk, he cried. I kept taking him to the doctor who could find nothing wrong, so I spent my days and nights cuddling a baby who didn't want to be pacified, and walked miles up and down a multi-coloured rug which danced in crazy spirals through the long hours of the night.

I eventually realised that the poor little child had colic, and after spending four or five hours every night with Peter's screams reverberating through my skull, it came as a relief to understand that the crying at least had a cause, and perhaps there was hope at the end.

When the time came for Adrian to leave for his placement, his parents, Bill and Dorothy, very kindly invited Peter and me to stay with them in Birmingham. I felt that this was an enormous intrusion upon their privacy, but they were so kind to offer that Peter and I bundled our way to their home shortly after Adrian's departure.

The weather was on the change. With late autumn came some piercing northerly winds which knocked you sideways as you trudged the pavements pushing a pram. I tried to keep up a routine with Peter so that he would feel settled and secure, but I still found that I was up three or four times a night to feed him and I felt wretched, homeless, rootless and missing Adrian more than words could say.

My confidence as a mother seemed to have evaporated. Everyone else seemed to be able to handle my baby better than I could. I wasn't sure how to introduce Peter to solid food as he reached 16 weeks, and my first attempts seemed feeble to say the least. I also felt that Peter's frequent crying was putting a strain on the household, so I would take him out for long walks each day just to give Bill and Dorothy a rest.

But I was so tired. I still couldn't sleep, and I was quietly going out of my mind with worry about Peter and Adrian. I tried to be a model daughter-in-law, but found it difficult to think straight about anything. I just wanted Adrian, but he was doing his placement in Sheffield, and we felt under the microscope. If we didn't cope well with this then there was always the threat of being removed from the training, and then we would have been homeless, jobless and completely lost.

The snows came early that year, and they came with a flourish. One Sunday morning it was impossible to drive to church because of the depth of the snow, so Dorothy and I carried Peter in his buggy all the way to church. I was so grateful to her for her willingness to do this, but in retrospect, I should perhaps have stayed at home with Peter and let them go to church in peace.

And then the whammy arrived. A few days later, I developed earache. At first I just thought that it was part of a cold, and then over the next day it progressed into an ear abscess. I didn't know where to put myself with the pain. The doctor prescribed some painkillers and antibiotics, but the next 48 hours were filled with indescribable pain. I kept taking the painkillers every two to three hours, which meant that I must have over-dosed several times, but I didn't care – the pain was worse than labour.

In this state I could no longer look after Peter, and I was reliant upon Dorothy to do that. Adrian's sister, Hazel, took the situation into her own hands and called Adrian, telling him that he needed to leave his place-ment and come back and look after Peter. I knew noth-ing of this until the call had been made. If Hazel had spoken to me beforehand I would have asked her not to ring. I knew that such action would be seen as a weakness on our part and that it could put our whole future with the college in jeopardy. But the damage was done, and Adrian arrived at his parents' home the following day.

I was so pleased to see him, but our joy was very short-lived as the following day we received a phone call from the family who were looking after our home in London. We had been burgled and the house had been ransacked. We drove down to London with a dreadful feeling of shock, anger and dread in the pit of our stomachs. How could anyone do such a thing?

As we entered the house I suddenly realised that most of my jewellery had been stolen. These were pieces which had been given to me over the years in Hong Kong. They were unique and irreplaceable and I felt that a part of my heritage had been ripped away from me whilst I was unable to do anything about it. I sat down on the bed surrounded by the contents of the chests of drawers. There was mess everywhere, and all our belongings lay strewn as though a tornado had burst uninvited and had left the room with the richest of pickings.

Adrian came into the room. "Oh Hil, this is awful."

What could I say? I sat dumbly looking at the remains of our belongings. We were interrupted by a knock at the door. It was the police, so we had to gather our wits and try to remember the items that we now knew were missing. I was angry with myself that I had not thought to take the jewellery with me up to Birmingham, but I had had too much on my mind to think of anything so sensible.

As we went through the list with the police officer, the cold hand of sadness gripped my heart. I knew that these were only things, but I still felt as though someone had violated me. Part of my history had been stolen. Part of my memories. I battled with anger and the desire to get even. Surely someone would find these pieces and return them to the police. They were so unusual with their oriental characters and beautiful stones.

As the police officer left, Adrian and I set about tidying the house and ensuring that the window which had been broken by the burglar was repaired. Then we had to return to Birmingham. It felt as though we were being knocked down and down. Only four months previously we had been riding the crest of the wave, and now we were shaken by one event after another.

We returned to Bill and Dorothy's tired and emotionally drained. This was all proving too much, but we had to persevere; we had no choice. Adrian contacted his tutor and went back to his placement for its remaining few days, and then we returned to London in readiness for the next module of his course.

All the time, though, we felt that we were playing catch-up. We knew that we had shown weakness in their eyes, and we knew that this was frowned upon, so we tried to cope with the rigours of the course without complaining. We might have managed if Peter had been more settled, but he continued to cry incessantly, and I was almost out of my mind with worry. My fragile self-confidence evaporated completely, and I knew that I was letting Adrian down by needing his help when he came home from college.

I forced myself to take Peter out for a walk each day and to keep the house clean and tidy. I tried to attend mother-and-baby groups regularly and to take part in the life of the college, but nothing seemed to take away the terrible feelings of failure which encroached upon my every waking moment, of which there were many. I knew that I should be happy. I had a wonderful husband who was following his call into Christian ministry, and I now had a beautiful son who was growing and developing so well. Yet, when a woman stopped to speak to me in the park and said, "These are the best days of your life", I nearly sobbed all over her. If these were the best days, then God help me.

It all came to a head one day when I was put in charge of supplying the teas and coffees at the local mother-and-baby group. I had been up most of the night with Peter, and Adrian was ill in bed with a stomach bug. I had bathed and dressed Peter and then dressed myself hurriedly and rushed out of the house to attend the group. I was busily trying to get my head around the orders for drinks at the group and suddenly realised that everyone was looking at my clothes. I looked down to find that the buttons on my shirt were done up incorrectly and that my dark sweatshirt was completely covered with milk stains. I looked like a tramp.

I returned home realising that I could not go on like this. I made an appointment to see the doctor, and sat in her office explaining the situation. "Do you think that you might be depressed, Hilary?" she said. For some reason, although I was a midwife and knew all about postnatal depression in theory, the thought that I might be suffering from it had never crossed my mind. I left her office clutching a prescription which I hoped and prayed would help to lift the terrible darkness which was completely enveloping my life.

It took time, but gradually I began to sleep better.

The terrible feeling of isolation and desperation gradually lifted and I began to feel more positive about being a mother. Adrian's course was continuing well, but there was a constant undercurrent of fear concerning our future. There was always a feeling that if we put a foot wrong, then we would be removed from the training.

I tried to accept the authority of the college, but it felt as though we were being forced to swallow something which was unpalatable. I had thought that a Christian organisation would show compassion and understanding to those who worked for them, but it was turning out to be the complete opposite here. Living under this sword of Damacles was a constant stress, but we did our very best to overcome each and every obstacle which presented itself. The awful thing was that we felt that we could not confide in anyone who had anything to do with the college. If we did, then news might leak back to the authorities that we were struggling. So we had to soldier on in silent anguish, praying that the Lord would give us the strength to cope.

Halfway through the training, the entire college was removed up to Sheffield, so we had to move once again, lock, stock and barrel. We were allocated a terraced house in the Crookes area of the city, and we were told that we were very privileged to be given a house in such an area.

As we drove into Sheffield early on that Saturday morning, we watched the busy skyline and set our hearts on this being our home, our springboard to our new future in ministry. We were excited and full of anticipation. We were following the Lord, no matter what it took, and there was a feeling of becoming a pioneer, as we were amongst the first students from the college to use their new and very handsome facilities.

We attended the local church, St Thomas's, which is renowned for its excellent teaching. In fact, it has a very large student population, and it catered for many hundreds of people. We introduced ourselves as students of the college, and were immediately welcomed warmly.

In the following weeks, we gradually found our way around the city. Adrian's studies continued and he worked hard, gaining creditable passes for his course work. His placements were also successful. His gifts with people of all ages made him a natural evangelist, and he had a way of speaking with people which brought down barriers and helped them to hear about Jesus. Not that he was pushy or opinionated – he always respected the other person's point of view, but he managed to convey his absolute faith in a wonderful God in a way which really spoke to people.

A couple of months after the move, I took Peter into town in his buggy. I had decided to walk because I liked a challenge, and Sheffield's hills do pose a significant challenge when one is pushing a buggy up them! After buying Peter a pair of shoes, I pushed him home, struggling all the way. My back was complaining as I turned the key in the lock, but I took no notice.

Later that evening, I felt very unwell and began vomiting. Unfortunately this had the effect of causing a slipped disc in my back, and I was rooted to the spot with a 16-month-old child hanging around my neck. I had to call Adrian back from a meeting, and then we were faced with the dilemma of whether we should contact his tutor or not. If we did, then this would again be seen as a sign of weakness by the college. If we didn't, then there was absolutely no way that I could look after Peter on my own.

We were desperate. We didn't really know anyone

in Sheffield well enough to ask if they could help us, so we had to contact the college and let them know the situation. As we feared, the news was not greeted with understanding. Instead we were criticised for not coping better. It felt as though another nail had been driven into our coffin. I was under strict instructions from my doctor not to bend or lift anything for three weeks, so, once again, we found ourselves in an impossible situation.

As I lay on my back in the bedroom, listening to Adrian's anguished voice as he spoke with his tutor on the phone, and hearing Peter's voice crying for me, I was once again forced to ask the Lord, *Why?* Tears of disappointment and frustration would not be assuaged. Why did it have to be this difficult? I was, in effect, pinned to the bed with the pain whilst I waited for the analgesia to take effect. I felt useless – worse than that, a millstone around Adrian's neck. He was doing a superhuman job as he pursued his training, and now he was lumbered with a horizontal wife and a baby who would not be pacified.

It all seemed too much. What could God be trying to teach us through all this? In my pain and fear, I found it impossible to hear anything clearly from Him. Instead, I felt crushed by my failings, and so alone and vulnerable. It seemed as though the Lord had taken us away from all our sources of support, our friends, family, work, and now we were being stripped of our confidence in the organisation which was supposed to be supporting us. Why had God led us to this place of desolation?

With great determination, we picked ourselves up and tried to carry on. I began looking after Peter again as soon as was humanly possible, but the pain was incredible. Adrian had to return to his course; he just had to. We tried to carry on as though all was well, and told ourselves that if we could just make it to the end of the course, then we would be freed to pursue the ministry to which God had called us.

At church, I became involved with the mother-and-baby groups and really enjoyed the opportunities to speak to women about the church and its mission in Crookes. We hosted a fellowship group at our house, which was attended by some incredibly intelligent and successful people. We felt like minnows in a very large pond, but we trusted that God knew what He was doing in appointing us leaders of such a group. We were neither academically nor materially successful. All that we could offer was our love for God and the truth of all that He had revealed of Himself through the events of our lives, together with Adrian's ability to open the scriptures. We had to believe that this would be enough. And we counted the months until our proposed release into ministry, which was due to take place in May.

In March, however, I began to feel sick, and a pregnancy test proved positive. We received the results from the doctor's surgery the day before Adrian was due to face the final assessment board. Our hopes were raised once again. Now, at last, we hoped, we would be riding high, and on our way to wherever the Lord chose to lead us. But things never seem to go that simply, and we were about to realise just how much of a detour God had in store for us.

Chapter Twenty-Two

The day after we received the news concerning my pregnancy, Adrian dressed himself in the college uniform and prepared for his final assessment interview.

"You've done so well to get this far," I said as he walked out of the door. "I'm so proud of you."

He smiled and stepped out into the spring sunshine, ready to meet his fate. I picked up Peter, put him into his buggy and took him for a walk to the park. I pushed the feelings of fear and dread to the back of my mind. The college wouldn't have let Adrian get this far with the course if they didn't intend to pass him, would they?

But at the back of my mind was this harrowing fear which had lingered with us ever since we had commenced training. All of the students' wives had constantly said that any one of us could be removed from the training at any time, and I felt a dread which would not be subdued with mere platitudes.

We spent all afternoon at the park. I kept looking at my watch. Adrian was due to have his interview at two o'clock and I prayed that the Lord would give him the words to speak, to answer the searching questions I knew he would be facing.

By 3:30, Peter was getting tired and it was time for

his nap, so I put him back in his buggy and walked home down the steep hills. I had hoped that Adrian would be returning home at about the same time, but the car wasn't outside the house, so I guessed that he must have been delayed.

I carried Peter up to his cot, settled him down and then went downstairs to make a cup of tea. By then it was four o'clock, and I was beginning to get very worried. In the pit of my stomach, I knew that something had gone wrong. But it couldn't have, surely. We had friends who were coming to babysit for us as we planned to go out to celebrate Adrian's success. There surely couldn't be anything wrong. Could there?

I prayed constantly. *Lord, You know all things. You know how wonderful a person Adrian is, and You have now given us this new baby to nurture. It can't have all gone wrong, can it?* I couldn't bear to listen for an answer. The knot in my stomach seemed to say it all. I paced up and down, up and down, not daring to call the college for fear of what they might say. Eventually, at five o'clock, Adrian returned. His face was ashen and strained with raw emotion.

"I'm so sorry, Hil," he gasped, "but I didn't make it."

I wrapped my arms around him as one would a small child. "It's okay, it's okay, everything is going to be okay." I kept repeating the words over and over again. In my heart I felt a numbness descend over my senses. What on earth were we going to do now? We had no job to fall back on in Sheffield, our accommodation was tied to the college and now we were expecting another baby. To complete the desperate scenario, it was the height of the recession of 1992, and jobs were extremely difficult to come by.

Destitution stared us squarely in the face. Not only that, but there was also the terrible sense of betrayal which we felt towards the college. It transpired that the woman who had interviewed Adrian had viewed him as a victim for her bullying for some time, and she had waited to demonstrate her power over him until this most crucial time. The bitterness I felt towards this woman was indescribable.

And yet we are told that we must forgive others if we are to receive forgiveness ourselves. But the raw emotions with which we were battling were too immense and too overwhelming to be subdued in a short time. We were shell-shocked, traumatised. We had passed from being successful Christians to a jobless family who were threatened with eviction in the space of one day. Our confidence in ourselves was strewn to the four winds, and it seemed that we could not trust the very ground upon which we stood.

We decided that we should appeal against the decision, and various meetings took place with members of the college staff. Adrian attended a second interview alone, and was told that the college would stand by its original decision. They offered us counselling, as though this would rebuild our shattered dreams and lives. Being of a feisty nature, I took full advantage of the sessions to vent my fury at the college and its practices. I think that the counsellor found it all slightly amusing. I'm glad that somebody found it so, because from where Adrian and I were standing, things were not looking too funny at all.

We were devastated. It wasn't simply a matter of becoming one of Britain's unfortunate jobless statistics, and in so doing, losing control of our lives; it was also the fact that we felt betrayed by a supposedly Christian organisation which had not only allowed a vindictive bully a free rein, but had also refused to accept anything that we could say in our defence.

We felt that the bottom had fallen out of our world. We had put our complete trust in God and now He had let this happen to us. How could that be? Surely a merciful God would not put His children through such rejection?

I wrestled with the dark emotions of fear and dread as though they were physical entities. My first thoughts in the morning were of plans to extricate us from this terrible mire, and throughout each day we tried to stay positive and focussed. We had to find a job so that we could support ourselves once again.

But the days turned into weeks which were filled with writing application forms for jobs of many descriptions. We waited for the postman with butter-flies in our stomachs. Perhaps today would be the day that would bring good news and offers of an interview. But rejection followed rejection, and Adrian and I filled the remainder of the days with the mundane activities of family life: washing, ironing, shopping and taking Peter to the park.

We tried to make life as happy for Peter as possible, but soon found that we didn't have enough money to buy new clothes for him. We shopped for food at the cheapest stores, and began rummaging in charity shops for whatever we could find to fit.

Through it all, my pride kept rearing its defiant head. I was not brought up for this. What on earth was I playing at? My story had turned into one of "riches to rags" – wasn't it supposed to be the other way around? But whatever we did, we couldn't find a way out of our situation. We were beginning to get desperate, and then the thing which all mothers dread happened. The washing machine blew up.

It was an old machine which we had bought second-hand before we left Dorney, and it chose to depart this world on a summer morning whilst I was doing the washing up. The explosion was so loud that it made Peter cry, and as I stood looking at its useless frame, I joined in with him. What were we going to do now?

Adrian and I tried to be positive about it. Perhaps we would be able to rent a washing machine, and in that way we could possibly afford another one, if we were very careful. As I removed the sodden clothes from the useless drum and set about rinsing all the clothes by hand, a silent, anguished prayer went heavenwards: *Lord, you know all things. Please help us.*

It's amazing how dependent we are upon all this technology. I was shocked by how much the washing machine's demise could influence my feelings of security. It was only a machine, and yet I felt as though yet another of my safety nets had been torn away. What was God trying to say? Why did He keep on tearing all our security away?

The rest of the day was spent walking around Crookes looking for second-hand washing machines and companies which might rent one to us. We saw one machine which was priced at £100. It was exactly what we needed, but we knew that we didn't have the money, and we could not realistically expect to receive it either. We came home tired and dejected. It had started to rain, and I suddenly realised that my shoe had developed a large hole in its sole and I spent the rest of the evening with a soggy foot. But God seemed silent and distant. Didn't He care that we were in this situation?

In a fit of pique I went upstairs to our bedroom

and knelt by the bed. I really needed to tell Him how unjust He was being. After all, if we hadn't followed His calling in the first place, we would have been living safely amongst our friends in Dorney and enjoying the success and prestige of Adrian's job.

Why have You brought us to this place, Lord? Don't You know what this situation is doing to us? Do You really want to destroy us? Why have You let this happen? And then there was only silence, and the silent desperation of my hot tears soaking the bedspread.

After a while, I went downstairs to join Adrian and Peter and we ate our evening meal, focussing on our little boy's needs and doing our best for the sake of him and one another. When Peter had gone to bed, Adrian and I sat quietly watching television. It helped to know that there was still a world out there where things happened to other people too, and that we were not the only ones who struggled with injustice, rejection and a very present cash flow problem. Our hearts went out to those who suffered. There is no glory in suffering. It is painful, humiliating and galling.

I found it very difficult to get any sleep that night. I kept worrying about washing machines and money, but in the morning we had to keep going, for Peter's sake. He didn't understand that our world had been completely up-ended, and that all our dreams of ministry had blown up in our faces. He didn't understand that we could not afford to buy him toys or new clothes, and that we had been brought down to the bottom of the economic pile.

But somewhere in the very core of my being, I felt a small voice reminding me that we were still children of the King. There was a small defiant part of me which told me to walk as a daughter of the Most High. We might be in a bad place at the moment, but we must hold on to the faith which we had been given. We must not turn our backs on God, because this was part of His plan for us, painful as it was.

As the post arrived that morning, I felt a leap of hope as I opened a white envelope. Inside, there was a building society cheque for £100. It had been sent anonymously by some wonderful Christian friend who must have been prompted by God to bless us in this way. They may never know what that gift meant to us.

The joy we felt was beyond words. We suddenly felt as though God, Who had been silent throughout the ordeal so far, had quietly spoken hope into our hearts again. He did understand what we were going through and He was providing a way for us to cope. We dressed quickly and went to the second-hand store to purchase the washing machine before anything else could happen to change our minds. It was delivered the next day and it stood in our kitchen as a beacon of hope, so that every time we were tempted to despair, we could look at it and remember that "Jehovah Jireh" – God is our provider.

In spite of this wonderful answer to prayer, however, I still battled with the sheer injustice of our position. Adrian had done nothing wrong, and the unfairness of the situation burned fiercely in my heart. At church, I felt as though we had slipped from a place of accept-ability to one where people were not quite sure how to approach us. Their thinking, I suppose, must have been that we must have done something terribly wrong to have failed the final assessment. The fact that we hadn't was something which we could not prove easily, so our predicament weighed heavily upon us whilst those around us surmised, and took a backward step.

We began to feel isolated amongst all these people who were so accomplished and successful. We felt it most keenly amongst those people who were supposed to be our closest friends, the members of the fellowship group. As the months progressed, I began to feel fearful of their judgement, and my confidence to lead the group dissipated. It was a vicious circle, and one which came to an unpleasant conclusion when I was asked to remove Peter from the meetings because he was causing the members to be distracted. I was ousted from my own living room, and Adrian was left to lead the group alone.

Adrian and I were under enormous pressure to cope with the situation. We were a long way from either of our parents and found ourselves ensnared in poverty, which was grinding us down. Adrian's parents then very wonderfully offered to keep our car on the road for us, and that indeed was a Godsend. At least we could get out from time to time.

But our health was beginning to suffer, too. Adrian developed an overactive thyroid gland which meant that he was under tremendous stress and his body was working far too quickly all the time. This also had the effect of making him feel very anxious and quick-tempered, and he would flare up easily and become very distressed. I think he is one of the few men in the world who can now identify with what it feels like to be premenstrual, and whilst it was an education in itself, it is not something that he would recommend!

I became desperate to find friends outside of our situation who would be able to understand and who could listen. The pain which we were enduring was becoming too difficult to bear. I feared for the future for us all, but especially for our unborn child. I felt so guilty to be bringing another child into a situation like this. I'm sure that members of our family were questioning our sanity for trying for another child before the outcome of the assessment had been made known. In one sense, I agreed with them, but in another, I had known that it was the right time to try for another child. It was as though God was trying to teach us to see things according to His plans, and not our own.

I found a friend in Jacky, who had a son who was a couple of months younger than Peter. She was a ray of sunshine and a rock in a storm. She would always welcome me into her home if she was in, and she would let Peter play with all of Ben's toys. Her husband, Jon, was in training at the college, and they never doubted our value or held our failure against us. For their constant love, patience and compassion, and their willingness to accept us as we were, I will always treasure them and thank God for them.

Another friend, whom I will call Tina, I met through the mother-and-toddler group. She also had a son who was a couple of months younger than Peter, and I would often pop round to see her. Tina was a wonderful person, so sweet and gentle and willing to listen, and I leant on her for support and help when I felt purposeless and without hope.

It came as a terrible shock one day, then, when she turned around and told me to leave her alone. I was devastated. I had never meant to overwhelm her with my problems. I had hoped that I had given her support and understanding in return for her friendship, but she said that she did not want me to visit her again. It felt as though the world had ended, and the slender strands of human support seemed to be snapping before our very eyes.

"I can't take much more of this," I sobbed at Adrian. "What are we going to do?"

We sat down and calmly considered the possibility of ending it all. We had reached the end of our endurance. There seemed to be no hope at all. We were completely spent – we had nothing left to give and there was no hope on the horizon. In desperation we felt that life was no longer worth living and that we had nothing left to offer our children. But for them, we might well have followed our intentions through, but the thought of bringing their lives to an end was too cruel. We couldn't do that.

So we continued in our grey half-life where the poor and hopeless, almost invisible, people dwell. We were beginning to know what it was to belong to that underclass which perturbs the politicians so much and whose members fill the seats in the doctors' surgeries. We signed on for Income Support, and I felt like a dirty rag as I sat in the plastic waiting room with my little boy in his second-hand clothes and my pregnancy for all to see. What must people think of us? Foolish, loafers, spongers, irresponsible? And all that we could say in our defence was that we had followed God's calling on our lives. It didn't feel like we were a very good advertisement for Christianity.

It's difficult to keep your sights raised heavenwards when you feel as though you are being ground into the dirt, but it was a daily discipline to do just that. Our daily routine continued to include a prayer time together in which we read the Bible. Sometimes the readings made me angry. They seemed to imply that all we had to do was pray and believe, and then all our problems would go away. At the same time there was a strong movement, originating in the United States, which professed that same belief. Our contempt for the "prosperity gospel" grew as our circumstances deteriorated.

But somehow, by the Grace of God, we hung on. I continued to take Peter to the mother-and-toddler groups at church, and Adrian completed one application form after another. Occasionally he would be called for an interview, and our hopes would be raised for the few preceding days, until news of the outcome reached us. Unfortunately, each time, he seemed to come second in the race for employment, and we would have to be strong for each other once again and believe that it didn't matter because God knew what he was doing, and He would reveal His plan to us at the right time.

In the meantime, we walked up and down the steep hills of Sheffield, and Peter learned all the names and makes of the cars which we passed. He was so bright and his language development was phenomenal for a little lad who was only just two years old. His progress gave us hope, and we concentrated all our efforts on supporting him. Everyone who met him commented on his vast vocabulary and understanding of the world around him.

But life was an act of will; there was very little which gave us spontaneous enjoyment. We had to set our minds on what was good, and concentrate on those things so that the difficulties didn't seem so significant. It felt like a spiritual marathon, in which one could not stop and indulge in self-pity or remorse. If we did that, then, like Peter trying to walk on the water, we would soon find ourselves overwhelmed by the waves of loss and poverty.

To feel vulnerable like this was painful in the extreme. We were at the mercy of our situation, not in charge of our destiny. My initial reaction had been to fight it, to try to regain some control over our lives, but as the months passed, that control gradually ebbed away and we found ourselves knocked back and forth by events. But we had to cling to Jesus. There was no other alternative. Either His words were true, and He could be depended upon totally, or we had been following a lie. It was crunch time.

As the time came for our next baby to be born we were made aware that our tenancy of the house would be under review. Although we were paying rent to the college, they had decided that we would have to think about finding alternative accommodation. We set about trying to find somewhere else to live, but were met with waiting lists which ran to ten years in duration. We could be homeless. We appealed to the college and they grudgingly agreed to extend our tenancy in the short term.

It was in this situation that I went into labour. Things began slowly on the Sunday morning, the first of November, the date the baby was due. We were so pleased that we had made it past Halloween. We went to the Northern General Hospital where I had booked for a water birth. As the sister watched the trace of the baby's heart, she commented that she thought that there could be a problem with the baby. Not again, surely. As the labour had not really established, I was admitted to the antenatal ward for observation and possible induction the following day.

In the meantime, however, I walked up and down the ward, and the labour became established. I prayed constantly that the Lord would bless this little child, and that if there was anything wrong with him or her, then He would sort it out. I felt that we had been

256

messed about too much and that Satan had really over-played his hand this time, and I was not going to stand for him attacking my child in this way. As I prayed, I felt an assurance that the Lord had heard me and that He would look after us both.

I was told that I would no longer be able to have a water birth, so I told Adrian that I was going to have a soak in the bath instead. Nobody realised, except me, that the labour was well under way at this stage. I sat in the bath for about an hour, and the warm water bliss-fully eased the pain. The only problem arose as the time came to get out of the bath. Suddenly the full intensity of the contractions became apparent, and I had to hop out of the bath and towel myself dry inbetween them.

"Could you tell the midwife that I need to get to the labour ward, Adrain?" I gasped. He dashed off in hot pursuit of a midwife, the notes and a wheelchair, and I clung onto the bath wondering if perhaps I had been a little too clever for my own good. I was left pant-ing and gasping and hanging onto the side of the bath.

When the midwife arrived, I tried to look cool and collected but the huffing and puffing which accompa-nied the contractions was a bit of a giveaway. I sat down gratefully in the wheelchair and suddenly felt very apprehensive as I realised that our journey would involve the use of a lift. I have never liked them. Perhaps it's because I have watched too much televi-sion, but I always have this terrible feeling that they are going to break down. In fact, one had broken down when I had been a student nurse in the process of trans-ferring a very poorly patient from Casualty to one of the medical wards. We had been trapped for about half an hour, during which time I had willed my patient to keep breathing.

Now, as we awaited the arrival of this metal chariot, I thought about the possibility of taking the stairs,
but another contraction began and it was as much as I
could manage to hang onto the arms of the chair and
not to moan. I was always brought up not to make a
spectacle of myself, so I carried on with the breathing
and relaxation exercises which were coming in very
handy.

Eventually, the lift arrived, and a large group of
visitors filed slowly past us. They were chatting amica-
bly and carrying flowers, chocolates and balloons. They
didn't seem to notice the woman in the wheelchair
whose eyes were bulging from the effort of concealing
advanced labour! As the chair was wheeled over the
metal rim of the lift I groaned inwardly. The action pre-
cipitated yet another contraction, and I spent the journey in our little metal box hanging onto Adrian's hand
and panting like a dog.

The midwife in charge of the chair took the hint,
and as soon as the lift doors opened, she wheeled me
post-haste through several sets of double doors and
down the labour ward corridor as though it was a race-
track.

"This is Mrs Cotterill ... " she began as she passed
the nurses' station.

Sister took one look. "Put her in Room 3." Hardly
slowing, my midwife cornered the chair to the right and
wheeled me into an old and rather decrepit delivery
room. I levered myself out of the chair and thanked my
chauffeuse enthusiastically, but then had to return to
the matter in hand, as another contraction came crashing onto the scene.

I clambered onto the bed and gratefully grabbed
the Entonox mask which was offered by Lilly, the mid-

wife, who had materialised from nowhere. I didn't wait to be given any instructions on how to use it, but began gulping in lungfuls of the stuff as quickly as possible. The valve on the cylinder was soon ringing and pinging as it had in the days at Welwyn, and I felt strangely comforted by this familiar sound. As the contraction subsided I grinned at Adrian. "This is great stuff; you really should give it a try!" He looked a little bemused, but our communication was interrupted by Lilly's insistence that I really should have an internal examination to assess the progress of the labour.

I felt tired and heavy and didn't want to move, but I wriggled up the bed and dutifully did as I was told. Before Lilly could begin her examination, another contraction began, and the room was filled with the hissing sound of the Entonox and the low moans which accompanied each exhalation. Lilly eventually found out that there wasn't far to go before I would be able to start pushing, so I spent the next three quarters of an hour sitting on the side of the bed, trying to consume an entire cylinder of Entonox as quickly as humanly possible.

And then it was time to push. Things had just got to the stage where I felt that I could not possibly endure any more pain, and Lilly kindly thought that I should add to this by pushing as hard as I possibly could. The baby's heart trace had been fine since we had transferred from the antenatal ward, and I thanked the Lord that He had heard my prayer. But as the second stage progressed, Lilly was concerned for the baby's welfare.

"Your baby is showing some signs of distress, Hilary. You are going to have to deliver him or her as quickly as possible." A second midwife came into the room. "Tell the registrar that we may need him in here for a forceps delivery."

My mind clicked into gear. I put all of my efforts into pushing this baby out, but even as I did so, I prayed for God's protection over this little child. And then, even in the middle of all the pain, worry and drama of it all, I saw in my mind's eye a little bundle of light. I knew that this was my baby and that he or she was being protected by Jesus. That image gave me an incredible peace, and as I continued to push, the baby's head began to become visible, and a couple of minutes later, he was born.

David was placed on my chest and we looked at each other. He looked straight into my eyes, and in that moment I felt an indescribable joy. He was beautiful, he was breathing perfectly normally and his colour was great. God had heard my prayer, and now this wonderful child, David Nathaniel (which means "beloved gift of God"), was lying peacefully in my arms.

It was as though all the struggles of the previous eight months were being nullified by this miracle. The joy of this most precious gift was perhaps made all the more special because of our terrible situation. Whatever it was, I felt as though this was the most wonderful thing in the whole world, and no matter how many other women gave birth, none of them could possibly be as happy as I was at that moment in time.

Out of a seemingly hopeless situation, God had chosen to give us this gift, and we were so thankful. How we would cope now that we had two young children, I could not tell, but for those precious hours which followed David's birth I felt as though somehow it was all meant to be, and that the God Who had protected my baby would find a way to shelter and protect us all.

Chapter Twenty-Three

The weeks that followed David's birth were shrouded in the greyness of sleep deprivation. He seemed to be perpetually hungry, in spite of the fact that he was getting liberal quantities of milk and was growing at a phenomenal rate. I began to empathise with the cows we would see ruminating soporifically in the fields, and would often be found staring into the middle distance whilst David suckled to his heart's content.

Peter was not too impressed with the newcomer initially, and I felt guilty that I was so protective of the new baby. Peter had been used to my almost undivided attention up until that point, and it was hard for him to constantly have his little brother occupying mummy's knee. My mother had told me that when a baby is born, you grow another heart, and I was beginning to see that the love we have for the first child does not have to diminish at all; we simply develop a whole new set of feelings for the next.

I suppose that is how God copes with the enormous demands which are made on Him. As people, I think that we find the concept of God's tremendous and individual love rather difficult to understand. From a logical point of view, I suppose this makes sense, but I believe that God's heart is very much a parent heart. He loves and understands each one of His precious children completely, and it doesn't matter how many billions of us that He has to deal with. He also has the added advantage of being outside of time's constrictions and can therefore always be with each and every one of us. And as a family, we were leaning rather heavily upon these promises.

Most babies seem to settle into a routine fairly quickly, and we were hoping that, because David was our second child and we knew a little bit more about parenting than we had first time around, we would manage to establish a routine sooner rather than later. Unfortunately, however, David hadn't read the script, and he continued to awaken every hour and a half, day and night, for the next eleven months!

By three months of age, he had doubled his not inconsiderable birth weight, and Adrian and I were developing biceps which a bodybuilder would have been proud to display. We would go shopping and I would wander around the aisles wondering what on earth we had come to buy, and having written a shopping list, would find that I had cleverly left it at home.

At about this time, I got up one morning and staggered downstairs to make a cup of tea, only to find the front door wide open. I thought that this was strange, as Adrian was still upstairs. An icy wind was blowing into the house, so I simply closed the door and scratched my head, trying to make sense of the situation. I called upstairs, "Adrain, have you been downstairs?"

A sleepy voice replied, "No. Why do you ask?"

"It's just that the door's open. I'm sure we didn't leave it open last night." And then the reality of the situation permeated the grey fog which lack of sleep imposes upon a person. A knot the size of a football leapt into action in my stomach and I ran into the living room, desperately hoping that I wouldn't find what I knew I would. Our video recorder, and my handbag, had been stolen.

The recorder had been a generous gift from the Riverside group of churches which had supported us when we left Dorney. We had bought it so that we could ensure that Peter had interesting things to watch while we were dashing around, and it was a bitter blow for this gift, which we had bought only two weeks previously, to be stolen.

We contacted the police, and they sent out an officer to check for fingerprints, but they seemed to have a good idea of who the culprit might be. Apparently this thief used long pliers to turn the keys inside the lock from the outside, and then simply came into the house and took whatever he wanted. It was a bitter blow. I had only kept the keys in the lock as a precaution to facilitate our escape from the house in the event of a fire. It seemed that our attempts to be as careful as possible had backfired in our faces.

We felt very sad. This was our second burglary in the space of two years, and this time we felt even more threatened. The thief had stolen into our home whilst we were there. He could have attacked any one of us in our sleep; in fact, I had probably been up feeding David at the time, but had no idea that he was there. It was a most disturbing thought, and all my maternal feelings of protection towards my children went into overdrive.

But it's an ill wind that blows nobody any good, as one of my teachers used to say, and our insurance company paid out for the losses, so it wasn't long before Peter was happily watching Thomas the Tank Engine once again. David, however, continued to be very hungry and wakeful. I kept reading all these articles about babies who slept for 19 hours a day, and wondered why mine wasn't keen to give it a try.

One night, I had had no sleep at all and it was heading for four o'clock in the morning. I had fed David for hours on end, and he had fallen asleep in my arms, but each time he felt himself being lifted into his cot, he woke up and began crying inconsolably once again. This had been going on for five hours, and I was running out of strength, stamina, milk, patience ... you name it, and I was out of it.

Adrian came into David's room. He had dark rings around his eyes – the badge of a new parent. "I'm sorry I woke you, Adrain, but he just won't sleep. I don't know what to do."

Adrian picked David up and walked up and down with him to see if this would settle him, but David continued to grizzle and complain. "Have you changed his nappy?"

"About four times, because of all the milk he's getting. I'm getting really tired now, Adrain, and I'm worried that my milk will dry up if I don't get some rest soon."

"Well, there's nothing for it, Sunshine. You and I are going out for a walk."

"It's only four in the morning, Adrain ... "

"I don't care. If it's the only way that we can get some sleep, then that's what we'll do." With that, Adrian put on some clothes over his pyjamas, and I scooped David into his little snowsuit and bundled him into his cosy buggy.

"I'll see you later, and mind you get some sleep." With that, Adrian and David strode off into the early morning, and I prayed that they would both be alright. I trudged upstairs and fell into an uneasy sleep.

About an hour later, I heard the front door open and the familiar sounds of the buggy being manoeuvred around the stair gate which protected Peter from the dangers of the kitchen. I held my breath, waiting for the sound of David's voice, but all was quiet.

Adrian came into the bedroom a couple of minutes later. "Are you okay, Adrain?"

He was laughing. "You'll never believe it, Hil, but I got stopped by the police!"

I sat up. "You did what? Were you speeding or something?"

"I was walking down Broomhill when a police car pulled up alongside. An officer wound down the window and said, 'Excuse me, sir, what are you doing pushing a pram at this time of the morning?' I explained that the baby wouldn't sleep and that I was trying to give my wife some rest. He had a glance in the buggy and saw that David was asleep and then he said, 'Very well, sir. That's fine.' I thought it was hilarious!" Adrian climbed back into bed, and we chuckled to ourselves for a few minutes. Was it us, or was our world going slightly squiffy at the moment?

It was events like these that helped us to laugh at our circumstances, and God knew that we needed humour from somewhere, because the reality of our situation continued to be very grey and grim. But as the sun pierces a heavy sky with shafts of sunlight, so His provision for us came in very precious ways. And one of those shafts of light and hope came in the form of Martin and Cath Stephens.

Adrian had first met Martin and Cath when they had attended an interview at the college, and there had been an immediate bond between them. Cath had been offered a place with Adrian, but after much prayer, she had decided that this was not the right course of action for her after all. Since those days in London, they had thought about taking over Adrian's position at Dorney, but then again, that was not quite what they wanted to do. They had, however, found a job working at a conference centre in Derbyshire which was about 35 miles from Sheffield, and we became very regular visitors to their warm and inviting home.

Martin and Cath became a lifeline for us. They were so kind and understanding. They never judged us and always welcomed us, and in those days when our self-confidence had virtually disappeared, their love for us gave us hope and a feeling of worth. They were God's provision on a very wonderful human scale, and their friendship helped to make our lives worth living. We are forever in their debt.

We would arrive at their home fraught with the stresses with which we were faced, and after taking a walk in the nearby fields, and marvelling at the beauty of Thorpe Cloud and Bunster Hill, and eating a meal together, our frazzled nerves would be soothed, calmed by the quiet and gentle care of two such lovely people.

Of course, nobody could give us the answer to the question which kept burning through our minds: *Why?* Why had this all happened to us? We hadn't done anything wrong, and yet we were still having to endure such uncertainty and feelings of powerlessness. Sometimes I would express my anger to Cath as we walked amongst the sheep. I wished that Jesus could be my good Shepherd right now, and come along and carry me close to His heart. Sometimes our pain is too intense for us to realise that He is doing just that. Perhaps it is during those times when we feel so alienated from Him by our circumstances that He is actually closest to us.

But I hadn't learned to distinguish the difference between that truth and the raw pain of rejection which threatened to be a wound that would never heal.

People who undergo interrogation often say that they can endure almost anything as long as they know that it will come to an end. The problem with our situation was that we had no idea if it ever would. But whilst our future seemed to be infinitely full of problems, our tenancy of the house was heading for a finite conclusion.

"We're sorry that you find yourselves in this situation," one of the college chiefs murmured as he sat in our living room. "But we do need the house for another family who are coming into training in September." He looked so smug, and it was all I could do not to spit out some vitriolic remark questioning anyone's sanity for wanting to join such an organisation in the first place. Instead, Adrian and I placed plastic smiles on our faces and nodded gravely as the colour in them drained away.

This was it then. We were going to be homeless as well as jobless. The axe which had been systematically chopping away at our security was going into hyperdrive, and before long, we would find ourselves housed in some bed-and-breakfast hotel with little hope of escape.

We wrestled hard with the feelings of panic which threatened to fizz out of control. We had to stay sane and focussed, for each other and especially for the children. We sent out urgent prayer requests to our friends down south, asking them to pray that we would find somewhere to live before the proposed date of our eviction. We felt like lifers on Death Row who, after years of pacing behind bars, suddenly realise that the moment of truth is upon them, and their pleas for clemency are falling on deaf ears. Where was God now?

It was at this time that the friendship of Gerry Pert became so real and meaningful. Gerry, like us, was enduring the incongruity of unemployment. He was a truly brilliant person, with great dignity, someone who, in spite of his circumstances, managed to put other people first. He would welcome people into church and make them feel special and wanted. He showed God's love for others by the gentle way in which he cared for them and spoke with them. He had learned to turn his own time of adversity into blessing for others.

One day, when Adrian and I had been getting worn out from disturbed nights with the baby and the constant demands of a two-year-old, Gerry arrived at the house and asked if he could take Peter out to pick blueberries on the moors surrounding Sheffield. I was anxious at first, but Adrian said that a break would do us all good. In fact, Peter had the most fabulous time and came home with blueberry juice all over his mouth and fingers.

Gerry would always welcome us into his home whenever we needed a break from our own four walls. An hour spent with him would somehow refresh and revive our flagging spirits. Gerry was one of God's most precious helpers, and a true anchor when we felt rootless and afraid.

And then, out of the blue, I was approached by one of the church leaders to lead a group of people in their first Alpha course. I was flabbergasted. Why would anyone ask me? My self-confidence was at an all-time low, I was practically moribund with sleep deprivation, and I was overweight from eating too many Mars bars in an attempt to keep my milk production high for 18 months. In fact, I was the last person anyone in their right mind should choose for such a job.

"He must be joking," I told Adrian as I replaced

the telephone receiver. "What on earth can he be thinking, asking me to lead a group? I can't do it, of course."

"Why not, Hil? This is a wonderful opportunity for you. You've been under our circumstances for far too long, weighed down by our situation and the demands of the children. God hasn't forgotten us, and this is an indication that He really believes in you. You can do it, and you'll do it so well."

Disbelief gradually gave way to the first stabs of sheer terror. Could I really do this? Did God really believe in me, after all that we had been through? I kept thinking of that Bible verse which says that God's strength shows up best in weak people, but kept arguing that He surely didn't mean someone as weak as me. I was on the bottom of the heap in almost every sense; how could He possibly work through someone like me?

The issue raised a multitude of feelings of worthlessness, and I realised that I needed to talk to someone who was spiritually mature and who was not directly involved in our situation. So I approached the counselling team at the church and was put in touch with a woman whom I shall call Deirdre.

At our first meeting, I was so relieved to be given this opportunity to talk to someone about how I felt, and how I was struggling to hear what God was trying to teach me through all of this. She seemed to listen attentively, but there was this little problem. She took hold of the fact that I had always felt so inadequate and proceeded to rather massacre the issue at each of our meetings. She then accused me of having the "Christian persona, but underneath, you are a very angry woman". Too right – that was exactly why I had come to her in the first place! I didn't think that I needed someone who had done a counselling course to tell me that. I was indeed furious with the college which had dragged us up and down the country and dumped us without any hope or justifiable reason. Wouldn't anyone be angry, especially when it was having such a detrimental effect upon one's husband and children?

I had come for counselling because I wanted someone to pray with me, to hear what the Lord was trying to teach me, someone to give me some hope, some purpose and some sense of direction. Instead, I found that we were stuck on the fact that I looked like a Christian but I was angry. Can't Christians be angry too? Especially when there is an injustice going on? As far as I could see, ours *was* an unjust situation, which Adrian and I were doing our best to handle with as much dignity as we could muster.

So, disappointed once again, I decided that counselling with Deirdre was perhaps not the most helpful of avenues. It seemed that wherever I sought refuge, someone or something would stand in the way. I attended a fellowship group for women with young children, which met on a Friday morning, and every week this group was taken over by a woman whose husband had left her. I was terribly sad for this woman, but week after week the entire two hours was spent talking to and praying for her, and none of us could get a word in. Whenever we offered her practical suggestions which could be helpful, she rejected them out of hand, and subsequently her situation never improved. But she was happy to absorb everyone else's love, time and energy. The group was being sapped of all its vibrancy and hope by one member, and in spite of my attempts to put others first, I found myself dreading Friday mornings. Yet there was nowhere else to go, and no money to do anything else with, and Adrian desperately needed a break from the children.

Everywhere I looked it was as though our situation, terrible as it was, was considered insignificant by others. Couldn't people see that we were dying inside? We had laid everything on the line to follow Jesus, and it had all gone wrong. Didn't anyone think that this might just be a little bit devastating? But I don't think that anyone at that time could understand the spiritual devastation which we felt, so we had to struggle on as best we could, hoping and praying that the God Whom we thought we knew could in all reality come through for us.

We were no longer walking by sight. Our security blankets, our hopes, our dreams had all been torn away. We were walking by faith alone now, and it was painful and dark, and felt very dangerous. We had to keep trusting that God would fulfil His purposes for our lives in spite of this seemingly pointless daily struggle, and that He would ultimately restore to us the years that the locusts had eaten.

So it was in this precarious state that I began my training as an Alpha group leader. As I attended the first meeting, I felt overawed by the quality of the other leaders. They were all high-achieving, professional people, and I sat at the back in my second-hand clothes, and shoes which still had holes in the soles. What was I doing in a place like this amongst people such as these?

I scribbled down notes, trying to gain as much help and guidance as possible, but in the pit of my stomach, I felt terrified. Supposing it all went wrong, and the group's discussions dried up with half an hour to go? What would I say to those people who asked really difficult questions about what it meant to be a Christian?

In all honesty, I couldn't say that being a follower of Jesus was easy. Becoming a Christian didn't mean that all our problems just disappeared, and it often meant that we were at odds with the opinions and ethos of those around us. All I could say was that knowing Jesus means that we finally know peace with God, and that living for Him gives a purpose and direction to our lives.

I left the training session and walked out into the sunshine feeling very weak and frail. Why did it always seem that the Lord wanted me to work from a place of such vulnerability? If He wanted me to be such a different person, wouldn't it have been far simpler for Him to have created me differently in the first place? With these thoughts mulling over in my mind, I trudged off down the hill towards our home. That was another issue. How long we would continue to call Crookes our home was something else entirely.

Chapter Twenty-Four

The afternoon before the first evening of the Alpha course was spent in close proximity to the bathroom. After a while, Adrian suggested that we go out for a drive to see if this would help to calm my nerves. We drove out to Peter's favourite "cold place" – Derwent Water – and had a short walk past the reservoir, and watched the sheep grazing peacefully.

We looked on as a very energetic farmer ran up and down some very steep hills in order to help shepherd his sheep into a pen. I was just explaining to Peter what a wonderful job this man was doing when he shouted across the field to us. "What the hell do you think you're looking at? Go away!"

I was most indignant. "I was just telling my son what a wonderful job you're doing, you stupid man!" I must admit that the last three words were said under my breath. We turned and walked sadly away. It seemed that there was even trouble in idyllic places like this.

"Why was that man so rude, mummy?"

"I don't know, Peter. Maybe he has lots of problems."

"He did look funny running up and down that hill – he was going faster than his dog!" Peter started laughing, and things seemed better. It did worry me that the entire mood of the family seemed to be constantly on a

273

knife edge. It took only a small adverse incident and the atmosphere could become explosive.

Just two days earlier, we had had such an episode. We'd had a bad night with David and we decided to visit Martin and Cath. On the way, I had expressed my concerns about the financial wisdom of travelling to Derbyshire when we had practically nothing left in the bank. Adrian had screeched the car to a halt, and then swung it around in the road, narrowly missing an oncoming car. He had then nailed the accelerator and shot off down a very narrow, twisting road at 70 miles an hour. I was terrified, and stared ahead, praying that God would protect us.

"Stop, Adrain, please stop!"

After a mile or so, he brought the car to a halt. "I can't do this any more, Hil!" He leapt out of the car and walked away. I was shaking as I slipped across into the driver's seat. We were about four or five miles from home.

"Are you alright, boys?"

Peter nodded dumbly and David was asleep. Thank God he hadn't been worried by what had just happened. I saw Adrian disappearing down the road, but I knew that he wasn't in a fit state to talk, so I decided to drive home. I didn't even know if Adrian would come home, and as I drove I had this awful emptiness in the pit of my stomach. What would happen if I never saw him again? How would I bring the boys up on my own and, more to the point, where would I bring them up? I could not impose upon my parents at this stage in their lives. The dreadfulness of the situation weighed heavily upon my heart, and once again that little word, *Why?* came screaming to the surface.

I carried David into the house, and Peter trotted alongside me. "Where's Daddy?"

"I don't know at the moment, Peter. But don't worry, we'll ask Jesus to look after him."

Peter closed his eyes and prayed, "Lord Jesus, please look after daddy and bring him home."

The innocence of his prayer pierced my heart. I was still trembling with the shock and indignation of Adrian's outburst, and I sat cuddling the children to me – more for my benefit than theirs. I forced myself to get on with routine things. I made some lunch for us all, fed David, sorted out the washing, anything which would stop me from having to think the unthinkable. Life was becoming unbearable. I felt overwhelmed almost beyond the point of despair. The only thing which was keeping us going was the fact that we trusted that God loved us and that we loved each other. If any part of the equation should fall apart, then there was nothing really worth going on for. If Adrian had decided that he was going to give up on us then there really wasn't any hope any more.

I tried to be brave, for the children's sake, and read them stories and played with their toys. All the while, my ears were straining for the sound of Adrian's key in the lock and the sound of his voice.

A few hours later, he arrived home, ashen-faced and with the look of a hunted animal around his eyes. His shoulders were stooped and he looked exhausted. I didn't quite know how to approach him. On the one hand, I was delighted to see the man I loved. But on the other, I was devastated that his driving could have killed us. We were on the ragged edge.

"Would you like something to eat?" I said.

"I'm sorry, Hil. I could have killed us all."

"I know."

He sat down in the dining room. I reached out to touch his shoulder. I so wanted to make everything better. "I didn't know where you were, or even if you would come home." I could feel the tears of relief, sadness, impotence and anger pricking the back of my eyes. He sat with his head bowed.

"Where else would I go?"

"I didn't know. That's why I was so worried."

"Are the boys alright?"

"They're fine. Peter was praying for you." A painful smile flickered across Adrian's face. He looked up.

"What are we going to do, Hil?"

I held him to me and stroked his head. "I don't know, Adrain. We just have to believe that God knows what He is doing, and that He will see us through this. We have to stay together on this; there is no other way. Either we believe God or we are lost."

Tears of reconciliation can be so sweet, but at the same time, the deep hurt caused by the college's rejection seemed to smart against our very souls. We moved into the living room and sat together as a family on the settee. It was important that we were close to one another, for it seemed that everything around us wanted to fragment us and drive us apart.

We put on a video of Thomas the Tank Engine and let the repetitive music soothe our very frazzled nerves. Perhaps there were still some good things left in the world, after all. A silent tear trickled down my face as I watched the back of Peter's little head as it bobbed up and down in time with the music. David awoke for another feed, and as the soporific hormones rushed into action and the milk began to flow, I prayed that God would hold us together and help us to be strong.

So it was in this state that I approached the Alpha course as a group leader. If only they knew, I thought, about all the weaknesses in my life, then they would never have chosen me to lead a group. But they had, and I found myself up at the church and talking to people I had never met at the meal which was provided at the beginning of each evening session.

Then we moved into the main worship area and Paddy, the course leader, began with his first talk about what it meant to be a Christian. There were a couple of worship songs, and then we split up into our groups. I felt sick with worry as we moved into our assigned area, and found myself grinning at everyone like a Cheshire cat on speed. I took several deep breaths and then launched into an introductory exercise which was supposed to help everyone relax and get to know one another a little better. I was relieved to find that I had been allocated two very mature Christians as part of my group, but there were others there who had only recently come to faith, and others still who were there to prove to themselves that there really was no God at all. An interesting mix of twelve people.

We worked our way through the questions on our sheet, and I was amazed to find that people actually began to talk. I sat and watched as members of the group opened up and expressed their feelings about life and God. Their participation was so candid and open. I began to realise just how much I needed to trust God more. I should have realised that this was His work, and that I didn't need to be terrified of everything going wrong. I felt a tremendous sense of peace, and yet the vibrancy of the Holy Spirit as He moved among us.

The evening came to an end, and I returned home full of excitement. Adrian was waiting for me and was so encouraged that it had gone so well. It took me hours to calm down enough to sleep, and even then, I was up four times in the night to attend to David. The following day, the spiritual backlash arrived. This so often happens when we begin to make progress in the spiritual realm. Anyone who says that we are not in a spiritual war has perhaps not come to understand the very nature of the enemy of our souls.

After the high of the previous night, everything seemed to go wrong. A huge electricity bill arrived in the morning post which left us wondering how on earth we were supposed to pay it. It transpired that an immersion switch had accidentally been left on for days, possibly weeks. Peter then fell off his bike and cut his lip badly, and David had one of those days when he howled whenever he was put down. Adrian had to attend the surgery for some blood test results, which showed that his thyroid was playing up again, and then, the *pièce de résistance*, I slipped a disc in my back.

Our doctor very kindly came out to see me and told me that I needed to rest. I grinned at her through gritted teeth. "It's a little difficult with these two," I said.

"Well, you must try. No lifting or bending for a couple of weeks."

I nodded obediently as my back went into another spasm, and tried not to gasp too much until she had left the room. Why did it always seem that whenever we made some progress, we were always knocked back? The spectre of gloom and defeat threatened to overwhelm us once again. Adrian had just started a computer course, and he had to telephone his instructors to explain that he had to stay at home to look after the children. It seemed that every time there was a glimmer of hope, it was snuffed out with incredible force. The temptation to give in to negativity was immense, but we knew that if we did, then the battle was lost.

Satan really wants us to be imprisoned by fear, pain, unforgiveness – all of these negative emotions which tear our souls apart – but Jesus came to set us free from Satan's power. If we believed in Him, then we had to stand upon the promises of the Bible. One of these is that God inhabits the praises of His people. So, if God is with those people who truly worship Him, then Satan's power is overthrown. So, we decided, when the spiritual battle became more intense, that this was a sign that we should begin praising God even more.

It may seem strange that we should start thanking God when everything is going pear-shaped, but it works. It does not come naturally to start singing when you feel that your life is in shreds at your feet, but when we begin to shift our focus from our circumstances, and then look up to find God's perspective, then the power of oppression is broken, and the joy of finding that God is with us in the very depths of our pain is even more wonderful.

Worship also had the effect of uniting our thoughts, and we began to feel recharged. Hope began to emerge, in spite of our situation, and our standing as children of the King of kings was re-affirmed. We were beginning to learn, perhaps very slowly, what it really means to be followers of Jesus. We were being made to face up to the truths which we professed every Sunday in church, and to take God at His word. We were beginning to know, first-hand, that God alone is our provider, and that every good thing comes from Him.

A few days later, I was hobbling around in a semi-upright position, trying to find some trousers for Peter that didn't have holes in the knees which hadn't been repaired endless times. But the only ones which fitted the description were about two inches too short. I sat on the edge of the bed and worked through Peter's entire wardrobe, but there was nothing left which could fit him properly. It was a similar situation in the jumper drawers. I felt the old foe, despair, tapping me on my shoulder, so I sighed and uttered a silent prayer. *You know, Lord. You know.*

About half an hour later, there was knock at the door and Catherine, a wonderfully faithful woman from the church, arrived with four carrier bags full of children's clothes. "I don't know if these will be of any use to you," she said, "but I was having a clear-out and you popped into my mind."

The clothes were perfect. They were just the right size and just the correct weight for the weather we were experiencing. We thanked Catherine from the bottom of our hearts, and we thanked God even more. He had been there in the moment of our need, and He knew our needs completely. We could never deserve such love and care, but He was giving it to us anyway.

Very slowly, we began to understand how our situation was teaching us precious things about the promises of God. These were things which we would not have learned if our path had been straightforward and easy. It was only by being put in this position of extreme vulnerability that we could truly say that God was being our provider, our answer to every desperate prayer, our Manna – Bread of Heaven. He was working through the generosity of family and friends to show us the intimacy of His knowledge of our needs, and how lovingly He could supply for them.

When the Israelites wandered in the desert for 40

years, not knowing where or when their journey would end, God alone provided food for them. God knew His people's needs exactly, and He provided for them accordingly.

But the people of Israel had to walk by faith, and they had to obey God's call in order to receive such blessing. In our own small way, we too were on a journey in the wilderness, and we were learning that God was our provider, every inch of the way. In much the same way, we did not know where our journey would take us, and it didn't feel like a picnic either, but we knew that we had to live what we believed, and trust that the Lord would uphold His side of the bargain.

Chapter Twenty-Five

The weekly Alpha course continued to be a challenge and, in spite of the fact that the Lord was undertaking in a most remarkable way, I continued to be very nervous prior to each meeting. It took me a very long time to realise that it was His work which was going on and that, in all reality, it wasn't up to me to control how well, or otherwise, the group sessions went. In some senses, I was just a very privileged bystander who could sit back and watch the wonderful ways in which Jesus was touching people's hearts as we worked through the big questions of life together.

The group members were very supportive of one another, and even the guy who had begun the course with the intention of proving to himself that there wasn't a God, found that his attitude had softened as he warmed to the truth that he was loved by a Being far more wonderful than words could say.

Towards the end of the course, there was a weekend session in which the ministry of the Holy Spirit was introduced. Now, to those who were new to all this spirituality, it could seem rather frightening to invite an invisible Being into close proximity and to experience some of His power. But Jesus referred to the Holy Spirit as a person, the Third Person of the Godhead, and Jesus explained that the Holy Spirit's ministry would be to help people to come to faith, and to empower them to do the sort of things that Jesus Himself did when He walked the earth with men and women. The Holy Spirit gives us an assurance that God is real and that He is with us, and His touch upon our lives reaches the very essence of our being, and quickens our very souls.

But it was with some trepidation that I approached the weekend. I could imagine our atheistic friend completely losing it and getting very disruptive. I also worried that I would not be sensitive enough to the Holy Spirit to understand what He was doing in the individual lives of the people in my group. It was another leap into the unknown, and one in which I had to trust that Jesus knew exactly what He was doing, and try very hard not to get in His way.

In the end, it turned out to be a wonderful time of blessing. For some, it was the beginning of a new life with Jesus. For others, it was a time when people were affirmed in their faith, and encouraged to keep going. For one woman, with whom I had the privilege to pray, it was a time of great healing and liberation, and I felt incredibly humbled to be with her as the Holy Spirit gently touched her. Her face was radiant with peace.

The entire worship area was filled with dynamic, creative energy as the Holy Spirit continued to minister to everyone present. Even those who were praying for others were touched powerfully, and it was a perfect demonstration of the generosity of a wonderful God. He always does things in such a way so that everyone will benefit.

For some, this weekend was acutely painful as people faced up to many negative feelings about themselves and their circumstances. As human beings, we are all flawed and broken. It is only as we begin to realise this fact that we can begin to open ourselves up to God and to recognise our great need of Him and, more importantly, His great love for us.

By the end of the weekend, I was exhausted and very relieved that it had all gone so well. I was so glad to get home and to relax at last. But relaxation was to be in short supply because there was still the huge problem of impending homelessness which hung over our heads. It seemed that no matter where we applied for housing, the waiting lists were enormous. We were facing the very real prospect of eviction. The thought of spending the indefinite future in a single room in a bed-and-breakfast hotel filled us with dread. How could it all have come to this?

The only way that we could make sense of our situation was to stay focussed on God's promises. In our daily readings, He kept saying that we should not be afraid, and that He was our provider. But as each day passed, and still there was no sign of a job or anywhere to live, our hope began to dwindle. We tried to be brave for one another, and for the children, and not to speak much of the fear which encroached upon our every waking moment. We hung on to the truths which we professed as Christians, and we agonisingly prayed that God would indeed be our provider, because we could no longer provide for ourselves.

The weeks moved on, and the college reminded us that we would need to vacate the house by the third week in August at the latest. We had already seen our friends commissioned for service, and had watched with heavy hearts as they had left and started new lives elsewhere. We felt very alone and vulnerable. If ever we needed God, then it was now.

And then, one evening, the telephone rang. It was

Adrian's mum. I only heard Adrian's side of the conversation, of course, but he was suddenly very animated. "No, we don't mind where it is – anywhere would be great ... At Saint Clement's? ... And when would it be available? ... I can't believe it! Wait 'til I tell Hil!" I heard the sound of the receiver being replaced and a moment later Adrian walked slowly into the room. He had that sort of stunned expression which one gets when there is a bolt from the blue.

"You'll never believe it," he said, and my heart leapt up and down from stomach to throat. "Mum's church's curate is leaving and isn't being replaced. Consequently, the house he's been living in is going to be vacant. The church have asked mum if we would like to rent it?"

We waltzed around the room laughing and hugging and shouting, "Thank You, Lord! We knew You could do it!" Suddenly, the dark incarceration of our time in Sheffield was coming to an end. There was light at the end of a two-and-a-half-year tunnel which was very dark and lonely. God was our provider. When we had nothing left, and no means of making things happen for ourselves, when we had come to the end of our ability to go on, then He had been there for us.

We now had something to aim for, and something to hope for, once again. Adrian still didn't have a job, but our move to Birmingham would herald a new beginning. We prayed for the finances to pay for our removals, and a very generous church member offered to pay this for us. We could hardly believe that at last we were being released from this truly awful time. A verse kept coming to me from the Bible which says, "I will bring them back from captivity", and at last, I began to feel that perhaps this was true.

As Adrian and I drove down to take our first look at the house prior to our move, I joked with him that I had never wanted to live in the Bahamas. It was a standing joke in our house, because before we moved to London, I had said that I had never wanted to live there, and then I had said that I had never wanted to live in the north of England either, and we had ended up there. And now, I thought if this was the way things worked in God's economy, if I said that I didn't want to live in the Bahamas, then hopefully He would send us there.

We drove on down the motorway, and then to our amusement we saw the road sign: "B'ham 36 miles".

"There you are, Hil!" Adrian said. "God is sending you to B'ham after all!"

When we arrived, we discovered the house was ideal for us, and we walked through its rooms imagining how it would look with all our motley furniture filling its corners and crevices. Father Christopher, who was vacating the house, led us from room to room, and his peaceful presence and gentle spirit soothed our whirring minds. We could see that this house was indeed God's provision for us, and that, although we were bruised and battle-weary from our treatment in Sheffield, God still had His hand upon us, and was working out His purposes.

We returned to Sheffield and made arrangements for our move to Birmingham in the third week in August. In the intervening weeks we rid ourselves of copious quantities of rubbish which had been quietly rusting in the wet cellar, and said our farewells to the true friends who had stuck by us through all our struggles.

On the day of our departure, we cleaned the house as all our furniture was carried into the removals van outside. Before closing the door for the last time, I took a look around in each of the rooms. We had come here in great hope that our life and ministry would flourish and develop. Instead we had known painful rejection and humiliation from the people whom we had trusted to open doors for us.

This was the house in which we had known the pain of desperation and the joy of reconciliation as our relationship had been tested to its limit by circumstances outside of our control. It was here that Peter had asked Jesus to come into his life, and here also that David had known his first home. In this living room, we had known times of wonderful fellowship when God had seemed so powerfully present, and it was here also that I had been excluded by a group of people with whom we were supposed to be friends.

As I shut the door for the last time, I looked up at the sky. It was dark with the threat of a summer storm. As I ran to the car, the first heavy drops of rain began to fall. Those drops reflected the pain and sadness of my heart for the time that we had lived in this place, but as we turned the car away, and headed down the hill in the direction of our new life, streams of sunlight poured through the clouds. God had carried us through this time of sorrow. He had been the Provider of our Manna, and now He was carrying us to a new adventure.